The New York Times

Sunday Crossword Puzzles

Selected & Edited by **Will Weng**

50 Sunday-Size Puzzles

Volume

I

TIMES

BOOKS

The two questions most frequently asked a puzzle editor are:

1. How long should it take to solve one of those large Sunday puzzles?

2. Is it cricket to use dictionaries and other reference works in solving a puzzle?

The answers are:

1. If you take pride in speed-of-solving you are missing a lot of fun. Crosswords are for relaxation and enjoyment, not for competitive oneupsmanship, so take all the time you want.

2. The crossword puzzle is each solver's own individual property, and the solver is welcome to do it any way he or she pleases. It is nobody's business how it is done.

Now with that in mind, it's time to settle down to a selection of fifty large puzzles that originally appeared in the Sunday *New York Times* . If you must fudge once in a while, the solutions are in the back of the book.

WILL WENG

Solutions to the puzzles are found at the back of the book.

ISBN O-8129-O67O-5

Manufactured in the United States of America
C987

Choice Words

by William A. Lewis Jr.

ACROSS

1. Winds
6. Somber shades
11. Embarrass
16. Outing
17. Pointless
18. Lost sight of
20. Most happy place
22. Griddle cake
24. Cover-up name
25. Revealed
26. London area
28. Shelter
29. Drying place
30. What company does
32. Melt off
33. Mention
34. Dawn goddess
35. Hails
37. Many times
38. Made with sections
39. Furtive ones
41. Cease
43. Kind of grove
44. Poker move
46. Three-abreast area in plane
47. Arias
48. Kiev comrade
51. Theory of behavior
56. Camel fabric
57. Deceptions
59. Glossed word
60. Pace
61. Good: Lat.
63. Pile
65. Useful things
67. Practice boxing
68. Too-too
70. Throng
72. Held
74. State: Abbr.
75. N.C. and S.C., for two
78. Congress in-betweens
80. Actress Fay
81. Farms
83. Writing Pere
84. Qualified
87. Atlantic republic
89. Sask. city
92. Be generous
93. —— Wednesday
94. Isn't alert
96. Cake
97. Skein
98. Holders
100. Bulls: Sp.
101. Number
102. Id ——
103. Show life
105. More: Mus.
106. Tuckered out
107. Send another way
109. Rural feature
112. Swift's home
113. Word of welcome
114. Fazes
115. Distance
116. Peace offering
117. Unreliable

DOWN

1. Police, postmen etc.
2. Map area
3. Places to stay
4. Not dark
5. Group
6. Weight-watcher's word
7. Items of interest
8. Take on
9. Massage
10. Helpful quality
11. Cause changes
12. Carried
13. Jejune
14. York's rank
15. Emergency wire
16. Centaur's home
19. Partner of totter
20. —— alive
21. Rich soil
23. Tall and thin
27. Spat
30. Caesar's enemy
31. Utah lilies
33. Pooches
35. Go rapidly
36. Slow one
38. Fly
40. Good rating
42. Group
43. Island dish
45. Pure pleasure
47. Not moving
48. Bans
49. Greek coins
50. Enthusiasm
52. Lover
53. What cannot be
54. Extra
55. Habits
58. Jotter's material
62. Illustrations
64. Hepburn sobriquet
66. Fastens
69. High abode
71. Is noisy
73. Greek communes
76. Squeal
77. View
79. Give
82. Annoying people
84. Attendant
85. Introduced
86. Child's outburst
87. Mother of Horus
88. Andrea ——
90. Forces
91. Shortened verb
93. Steve, Woody, etc.
95. Old oath
98. Pin-up girl
99. Office worker
101. Fail
103. Attraction
104. Uses up
106. Color
108. Japanese item
110. Letter
111. Companion of dit.
86. gradually

Stepquote

by Eugene T. Maleska

ACROSS

1. Start of an eight-word quote descending in stairstep fashion to 150 Across
7. Small-time operator
13. Parnassians
18. Road job
19. Crisp cracker
20. Soirees
22. Gets one's bearings
23. Franken heroine
24. Chilean desert
25. Money player
26. Bach opus
28. Exceeded the resources of
30. Needlefish
31. Standstill
33. —— Gay, historic plane
34. Trifling
35. Together
37. Took pleasure in
39. Part of Stepquote
42. B'way group
43. Sweeten the pot
44. Proven
46. Put in relief
48. Utter
49. Author of Stepquote
50. Bills
52. Roundabout way
54. Construct
56. D-Day vessel
57. Certain rummy cards
60. Moved swiftly
62. Mind over platter
64. Science fiction site
65. Social asset
67. Hits hard
69. Raid
73. Eastern title
74. Very funny!
76. Actress Massey
77. Turkish city
78. Zero
80. Stubborn
83. Southern France
84. Prayer
86. Part of an antler
87. Tupelo or wicopy
88. Family member
89. Rich repasts
90. Knitted cape
92. Whoop
94. Mailed
95. Sweetsop
97. Printers' double daggers
99. Geological period
101. Cold cubes
104. Sheep
106. Hags
108. Sullen
109. David's daughter
111. A.M.A. members
113. Gide's "—— Is the Gate"
115. Figures of speech
119. Turkish standard
120. Man-made lake
122. Part of Stepquote
124. —— umber
125. Opp. of fortis
127. Fervent
129. Partner of fish
131. Utah flower
132. Neither Dem. nor Rep.
133. Do-it-yourself man
136. Shouts
138. D.C. group
139. Unyielding
141. End of a K.O. count
143. Krypton, for one
145. Indigenous group
146. Dodgers
147. Rank symbols
148. Ballerina Jeanmaire
149. Perceives
150. End of Stepquote

DOWN

1. Tell
2. Memorial Stadium team
3. Three in Roma
4. Hence: Latin
5. —— dark
6. Part of Stepquote
7. Stabilized
8. Gums
9. Very short pencil
10. Trapper's cache
11. Mystery
12. Ronald and family
13. Moderate
14. Tilled land
15. Army group: Abbr.
16. Twill weave
17. Of word meanings
18. Items for heads with tails
19. Cooked, in a way
20. Reinvested stakes
21. U.S. painter
27. Some Richards
29. Place for a frontal
32. Coaches
36. Principle
38. Ivy League team
40. Rosters
41. Part of Stepquote
45. Part of O.T.
47. Vain
49. Tire mark
51. Famous southpaw
53. Wry reply
55. Intended
57. Sir Rabindranath
58. Sister of Clio
59. Steep slopes
61. Tenfold
63. Shipshape
64. —— few words
66. Symbol of discipline
68. Glossy fabric
70. Gone up
71. Water nymph
72. Follower of a belief
75. Not forming an angle
79. Artificial satellite
80. Take out stitches
81. Makes a debut
82. Sniggled
85. Coat fur
91. Category
93. Boodle
94. Like an antitoxin
96. Parts
98. Customs officers
100. Check
101. Romance language
102. "Pudd'nhead Wilson's ——," source of Stepquote
103. Correct mss.
105. Hold forth
107. Draws off
110. "What —— bid?"
112. Russian length units
114. European linden
116. Maxim
117. Airport roarers
118. Ermines in brown
121. Infer
123. Part of Stepquote
126. Rung
128. French writer: 1823-92
130. Adriatic island
134. Arrow poison
135. Colors
137. Belgradian
140. Sixty secs
142. Kickoff gadget
144. Twice DI

Changing World
by William Lutwiniak

ACROSS

1. Quagmires
5. Tincture
10. Outer wear
14. Right-hand man: Abbr.
18. Quiz
19. Originate
20. Angel gear
21. Tete- ——
22. Annual phenome-non
25. Bucephalus
26. Application
27. Exclusively
28. Disentangle
29. Perplexes
30. Denials
31. Garagemen: Abbr.
32. French city
33. Bantu-speaking Africans
36. Swiss city
37. Open-air
41. Peak in the Cascades
42. Checker-berry
44. City on the Danube
45. Lamp item
46. Como or Garda
47. Turkish titles
48. Character in "Peter Pan"
49. Hooter
50. Like some fruits at times
54. Man —— (entre nous)
55. Nursery item
57. Eyes: Slang
58. Hall of ——
59. Gaffe
60. Pay
61. Glove man
62. Whitens
64. Turnstile item
65. Pastry
68. Competi-tions
69. Gymnastic feats
71. —— shoe-string
72. Signs, informally
73. —— -Co-burg
74. Gatherings
75. Qualifying words
76. Farm sound
77. City on the Sangamon
81. Bullish times
82. Irregular ode
84. Fissures
85. Salad item
86. "Dear me!"
87. Hacienda features
88. Punch: Colloq.
89. Storied ship
92. Attack
93. Blue-green
94. Bleacherite
97. Small amount
98. Do the unexpected
101. Simulated
102. Greensward
103. Clerical leave
104. W.W. II powers
105. Jefferson
106. Two- —— (in theater)
107. Cons
108. Witticism

DOWN

1. Escort
2. Amu Darya
3. Attendance
4. Dallas campus
5. French resort
6. Some tests
7. Flower
8. Adjective ending
9. Application
10. Whence's companion
11. Eastern VIPs
12. Amaryllis's cousin
13. Small, for one
14. Adjust
15. Appear
16. One or goose
17. Williams and Ken-nedy
21. To the rear
23. Wastelands
24. Family member
29. Vaults
30. Halo
31. —— letters
32. Do house-work
33. Skewer item
34. Town south of Asmara
35. Resorts to
36. Narrow-minded one
37. Greek city
38. Vacation place
39. Unclouded
40. Straws in the wind
42. Oasis feature
43. Shows
46. Crescents
48. Endings with three and four
50. Sty noises
51. Assuage
52. Zealous
53. Closing words
54. Prepares to take off
56. Shoe parts
58. Typesetter's concerns
60. Some voters
61. Packaged
62. Pleat
63. City of Vietnam
64. Virulent
65. Contests
66. Put down
67. Talking back
69. Lucknow wear
70. Aids'
73. Sprinkle
75. Bamboozle
77. Seasoned
78. Delight
79. Lawbreaker
80. Heatedly
81. Digest
83. Habaneras
85. Woos
87. Sawlike part
88. Military group
89. Vessel
90. Painful word
91. Preposition
92. Idaho
93. Sailing
94. Prix ——
95. In present condition
96. Hotbed
98. Location: Abbr.
99. Tool
100. Reign, in India
companion

4 Literally Speaking

by Anthony Morse

ACROSS

1. Gold or copper
6. Rib
11. Hold up
16. Mme. de ——
21. Fresh air
22. Chose
23. Uneven
24. Fenetre's relative
25. Applause in Yankee Stadium
27. Irritated archer
29. Conn. name
30. Red Square name
31. Embed
32. Stays in place, as a ship
33. Peer
34. Labor name
35. Alhambra room
36. Clasp
40. Minimum
41. Noted contralto
45. City on the Somme
46. Misstaters
47. Gray color
48. Girl's name
49. Parts of insects' jaws
50. Warning signal conks out
53. Cards
54. Latin phrase
55. Hot spots
56. Slips
57. French numeral
58. Largest digit
59. Sheer linen
60. Thin disk
62. Miss Starr
63. Clock setting: Abbr.
64. Certain Roman ruins
66. Clarence's cousin
67. Radar spot
69. Light-Horse Harry
70. Hero in Greek legend
71. Horse
73. Flexible span
80. Oriental pagoda
83. '49 gold rush name
84. Type of flu
85. Sudden move
86. Blanc
87. Warsaw people
88. Asian VIPs
89. Central
90. Andrea del ——
91. Brain passage
92. Drama school teachers
95. Fibers
96. Poetic word
97. Intervening: Law
98. Duplicate
99. Polynesian skirts
100. Scorned
102. Mixes
103. Personality plus
105. Former dog star
106. Western resort
107. Refuse
108. Malevolence
111. Greek island
112. Reluctant
113. Photo of a kind
117. Where to find an almond
119. Mute domestics
121. C'est ——
122. Evangelist McPherson
123. Island west of Curacao
124. Radio's Baby Snooks
125. Put right
126. Reuners
127. Bremen's river
128. Low point

DOWN

1. A Dick
2. Pound
3. Dupe
4. English queen
5. Word book: Abbr.
6. Stick
7. —— shut
8. Author Gertrude
9. Bird
10. Commercials
11. Not comme il faut
12. Wandering
13. Goofy
14. Aide: Abbr.
15. Favorable word
16. Fly in the ointment
17. "I haven't got a thing ——"
18. Weapons
19. French political unit
20. Fabric
26. Groups
28. Men about town
31. Buck or Bailey
33. Pulitzer Prize poet, 1929.
34. Grocery sign
35. Cuts
36. One of the Four Horsemen
37. —— of Gaul
38. Mute domestics
39. Kid
40. Attend a lecture
41. Seeds
42. Sequels
43. New York lake
44. Winter resort
46. Thread
47. Up ——
50. Australian export
51. Salute
52. Clockmaker Thomas
53. Field of activity
57. England's lifeblood
59. Candle
60. Doll up
61. Tree genus
62. Bounty man
64. Penalties
65. Spanish duke
68. About 61 cubic inches
71. Spotted
72. Shake-speare, very often
73. "...to a —— a bone..."
74. Custom
75. Alpine wind
76. City map areas
77. Lace trimming
78. Rages: Latin
79. Legal degrees: Abbr.
81. Sinus cavity
82. Mother of Xerxes
86. Polynesian
88. Mixed up
89. Make: Fr.
90. Marks
92. Sonnet part
93. Opening for pets
94. Mixtures
97. Botched a pool shot
99. Turkish title
101. ——
102. Departed
103. An early Tarzan
104. Shooting affair
106. Topic of discourse
107. Home, in old Rome
108. Ryun's distance
109. Former Asian kingdom
110. Wash
111. Type of pine
112. Fly or feather
113. Code word for a letter
114. Whitelaw ——, journalist
115. Bow: Prefix
116. Belgian river
118. Long Island harbor
119. Blackbird
120. —— Saud

Word Weaving

by Jack Luzzatto

ACROSS

1. Let off
7. Short of
13. Italian foods
19. From office boy to boss
20. Expert teaser
22. Eastern Christian
23. Philosophic doctrines
24. Cupboard
25. Surveyor's helpers
26. Wander
27. Creator of Hans Castorp
29. Finery
31. Degrees
32. Old measure
33. Less taxing
35. Fastener
36. Eleonora
37. Condescend
39. Capek
41. Corrupts
43. Peaks
45. Wrap in waxed cloth
47. Tidy
48. Flew in a way
50. Purvey
51. Finishing touches
55. Settled up
56. Computer word
59. Girl's name
60. —— tenens (stand-in)
62. "Make thee —— of gopher wood"
63. Mother-of-pearl
64. Farewell: Lat.
66. Common effort
69. Box of a kind
70. Off center
72. With: Scot.
73. Column style
75. Associate of Phiz
76. Top men
79. Plane wing support
81. Of deserts
82. Girl's name
83. Opera heroes
84. Large birds
86. Vegetable
87. Given by word
88. Restore
92. U.S.

violinist
94. Axe mark
98. "Go Tell —— Rhody"
99. An Allen
101. Brings to mind
103. Arctic explorer
104. Man's name
105. Expressed contempt
107. Gone
108. Bean
109. Gossip, down South
111. "The —— Worker"
113. Lawless one
115. Patterns for tracing
116. Grudging
117. Interpolate
118. Gives pause
119. Deeds
120. Lost sheep

DOWN

1. Made points
2. Release, in a way
3. Wild sheep
4. 500 sheets
5. Poetic dusk
6. Tense state
7. Deceitful one
8. "Camelot" librettist
9. —— sahib
10. Repute
11. More crafty
12. Equivocation
13. Strict
14. Buffalo's cousin
15. A Caesar
16. Jewish month
17. Relaxed
18. Five ——
21. Plunder, old style
28. Questioned
30. Eye part
33. Wind
34. News summary
36. Type of computer
38. Festivity
40. Makes dull
42. Roman poet
44. French claret
46. Queen: Sp.
48. More dignified
49. Iridescent
50. Pilot's concern
52. Islands in

Bay of Bengal
53. Stheno et al.
54. Pepper effect
55. Devastate
56. Finland, to the Finns
57. Musketeers and others
58. Image
61. Form of carbon
65. In one's ——
67. Follow
68. More fussy
71. Adjusts sails
74. Church laws
77. Perspicacity
78. Having a dull finish
80. Machete

83. Japanese verse form
85. Overstuff
87. Ability
88. Poured
89. Gibraltar to Lapland
90. Getting nowhere
91. Topic
93. Appraise
95. Not so fresh
96. Steichen's eye
97. Sincere
100. Audacity
102. High perch
105. Suffix with gang or mob
106. Platform
108. Asea
110. Exist
112. Small house
114. Political winners

Quotations

by Hume R. Craft

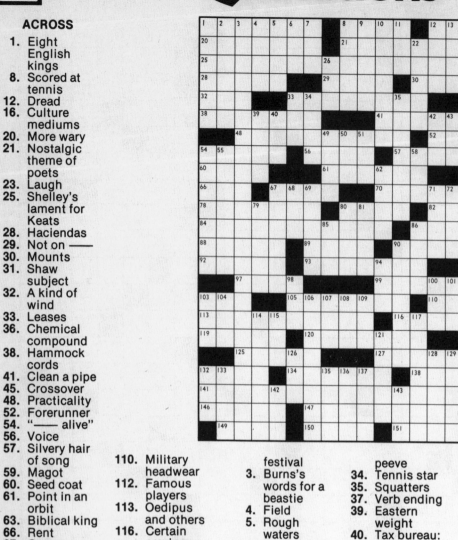

ACROSS

1. Eight English kings
8. Scored at tennis
12. Dread
16. Culture mediums
20. More wary
21. Nostalgic theme of poets
23. Laugh
25. Shelley's lament for Keats
28. Haciendas
29. Not on ——
30. Mounts
31. Shaw subject
32. A kind of wind
33. Leases
36. Chemical compound
38. Hammock cords
41. Clean a pipe
45. Crossover
48. Practicality
52. Forerunner
54. "—— alive"
56. Voice
57. Silvery hair of song
59. Magot
60. Seed coat
61. Point in an orbit
63. Biblical king
66. Rent
67. Goes to court
70. Quixote, et al.
75. Gels
78. Warning signals
80. Hipsters
82. Patsy
83. Kentucky school
84. Certain growths
86. Censured
88. Sounding made by radar
89. Medley
90. French painter
91. Bode
92. Suiting
93. Large basket
95. Lee's men
96. Indian reed
97. It —— laugh
99. Finger lake
102. Staple
103. Bristle
105. Exported
110. Military headwear
112. Famous players
113. Oedipus and others
116. Certain craving
119. Attempts
120. Legendary ivory statue
122. Lover of beauty
125. Lucifer
127. Ring men, familiarly
131. Rodent
132. Spin: Scot.
134. Command
138. Beginning golfer
139. —— as a fiddle
141. Tennyson title
146. Leads
147. Lords it over
148. Sentimental talk
149. East: Sp.
150. N.C. college
151. Or ——
152. Sioux

DOWN

1. Call forth
2. Hindu festival
3. Burns's words for a beastie
4. Field
5. Rough waters
6. Crossword clue: Abbr.
7. Broadway sign
8. Whaling man and others
9. Electronic device
10. Ham actors
11. TV room
12. Verb for Tinkerbell
13. Comfort
14. Pine
15. Double-checked mss.
16. Prepositions
17. Insects
18. Campion title
19. Coal deposit
22. Italian food
24. Sullivan and Begley
26. Beta or gamma
27. Theory
33. Kind of peeve
34. Tennis star
35. Squatters
37. Verb ending
39. Eastern weight
40. Tax bureau: Abbr.
42. Damage
43. Digit
44. Hagen
46. Droop
47. Poet's word
49. "—— giddy as . . ."
50. Small drink
51. W. W. II area
53. Civil War initials
54. Users of cellars
55. Small spaces
58. Pronoun
62. Organizes (with up)
64. Zoroastrians
65. Spy
67. Small seal
68. —— corda (soft pedal)
69. Bar
71. Field: Lat.
72. Slangy negative
73. Road surface
74. Petiole
76. Perform again
77. Cowboy gear
79. Drags: Colloq.
80. Quarter
81. Shortly
85. Pier union: Abbr.
86. Actor Calhoun
87. Unruly group
90. Lacus Asphaltites
94. Bartender's rocks
95. Engrossed
98. Vibrate: Abbr.
100. Musical instrument
101. Horse talk
102. Baseball name
103. Quick-witted
104. Price ——
106. Climax
107. Lupino
108. Clay: Prefix
109. Biblical song: Abbr.
111. Appian Way
112. Hollywood area
114. Soaking, and no kidding
115. Adherent: Suffix
117. Ne'er-do-well
118. Wartime agency
121. Made of wood
123. Cutting: Fr.
124. Scotsman's aims
126. Word after hand or horse
128. Chars
129. Camera glass: Var.
130. Bird
132. Army man: Abbr.
133. "Winnie —— Pu"
135. Organic compound
136. Earth's envelope: Abbr.
137. Climb
139. Middle East port
140. Triple or homer
142. Noun suffix
143. Before dee
144. "—— a deal!"
145. Time period

Guess Who

by Betty Leary

ACROSS

1. Renounce
7. Actress Elsie
12. Egyptian goddess
16. Beak
19. Smallest ones
20. Turn outward
21. Easily done
23. Biblical name
24. Presiders
25. Toy
27. Folios: Abbr.
28. Fuel
29. Shell
30. Place
31. Purposeful
33. Appendage
34. To the ——
36. Constructed: Abbr.
37. Nonsense!
38. Pearl Buck heroine
39. Second-rate
41. Elm fruit
43. "Come —— faithful"
44. Halo
45. Style of fiction
48. Iowa town
50. Tasted, in a way
52. Any of the Furies
53. Hair style
55. Constellation
56. Desk item
57. Pedestal parts
59. Poison tree
61. Cooked
63. Bower
65. Waterfall: Scot.
66. Packaged, in a way
68. Like Prospero and Miranda
69. Adjective suffix
70. Old Dutch measures
72. Long-legged birds
74. Pawns
75. Huckster
78. Business abbreviation
79. Cut ——
83. Glossy lacquer
84. People of rank
87. Algerian city
88. Suffix with block and brig
89. Bounce
90. Archeology finds
91. Pronoun
93. Fenced areas: Abbr.
95. Race horse
96. Vehicle
97. Sounds from the gallery
99. Turkish weights
100. Haven
101. Frenchman's roof
103. Basket material
106. Texas city
108. Garment
110. Cornbread
112. Couple
113. Informal wear
115. Canadian physician and others
116. Busybody
120. Math abbreviation
121. French adjective
123. Orchestra section: Abbr.
124. Walls in
125. Etruscan title
126. Occupied
127. Rome, to Caesar
129. Signify
130. Can. province
131. 1002
132. All
135. Opening in a game
137. Half boot
138. Staves off
139. Slow learner
140. Eliminate
141. Sign, informally
142. Shaggy dog
143. Advantage
144. Stopped over

DOWN

1. One of the Furies
2. Lament
3. Advice from Mother Goose
4. Recipient
5. Road map entry
6. Letter
7. Flat
8. Sailor's call
9. Connecting part
10. Annoy
11. Refinery worker
12. Arid wastes
13. Acid prefix
14. Lhasa's site
15. Workers' group: Abbr.
16. Part of an adage
17. Maneuvered
18. Pear
21. U.S. agency
22. Laud
26. Public officer
29. Pronoun
32. Fitzgerald
34. Splendor
35. Round
36. Bull form of Ra
40. Congo animal
41. Warning devices
42. Consequence
43. College title: Abbr.
45. Laborer
46. Campus area
47. Good times
49. Woeful
50. Biblical wife
51. German philosopher (1855-1941)
54. Disgusting
56. Not clerical
58. Price cut: Abbr.
60. 100 centavos
62. Turpentine resins
64. Harmony
66. Chits
67. Der ——
68. Eastern college
71. In ——
73. British subway
74. —— around
76. Swiss river
77. Fort in Kentucky
80. Pros
81. Just sits
82. Good queen
85. Steak garnish
86. Goldbricks
89. Palmetto State native
90. English spa
92. To be: Lat.
94. Hale's Philip ——
95. Golf term
96. Spanish uncle
97. Sits in judgment
98. First name in Dogpatch
102. Football's Simpson et al.
104. Girl of song
105. Shaggy dogs
107. Legendary king and others
109. Times of day
111. Words for a poor dresser
114. Notions in Paris
116. Trembled
117. Container
118. Indian in America
119. Boxed
121. Make oneself heard
122. In good time
124. Goal
126. Kaffir warriors
128. Abbreviation in rental ads
129. Teenage hairdo
130. Abbess
133. Certain verbs: Abbr.
134. Project
135. Weight units: Abbr.
136. Of age: Lat.

In the Old Sod

by A. J. Santora

ACROSS

1. Town near Salerno
6. In cipher
11. Years
15. Kneehole
19. Nikolai
20. Knowing
21. Extinguish
22. Matrimony
23. "—— look at it"
24. 1835 novel
26. ——prinz (Ger. title)
27. Feel pity
28. Zigzag
29. Knowing
31. Nobel physicist, 1925
33. —— majesty
34. Children's writer
36. Halberd and battle-ax
39. Cables
41. I hate: Lat.
42. Spells
44. Parhelion
45. Flamboy- ance
49. Journey
50. Belgian town
51. Urey, for one
53. Streaked, as wood
54. That is: Lat.
56. Iconoclast's opposite
58. Go-go dancer of myth
60. Reagan, for short
61. Item
63. With
64. Belgian shoe
66. Foxy
67. Dairy case item
70. Japanese apricot
73. ——-brac
74. Poetic start
75. Prepo- sitions
76. Easily shifted: Abbr.
79. Jitters
81. Pears' cousins
84. Crown
86. Federal group: Abbr.
87. Sets in an order
89. Warsaw for one: Abbr.
91. Kosygin's no
92. Like some satellites
94. Home: Abbr.
95. Big leagues
97. Month: Abbr.
98. Northern ——
100. Autocratic
101. Freely, in music
103. End of the loaf
105. Rule: Fr.
107. Record player
108. Nun of an order
112. Color
114. Arabian Nights' total
115. Light overcoat
117. Shore
118. Compo- sition
119. Good taste
120. —— water
121. —— curiae
122. Verse man
123. Injection, familiarly
124. Prows
125. Followings

DOWN

1. Raines
2. Nut tree
3. Ready to putt
4. Some poems
5. Like: Suffix
6. Rome's "censor"
7. Man ——
8. Beclouds
9. Clears a tape
10. Blood rels
11. Together, in music
12. Bay of song
13. Envoy's home: Abbr.
14. Burst
15. Medic of films
16. Reconcilia- tions
17. Blarney
18. U.S. artist
25. Type of watch spring
28. Bosses
30. Shoot
32. Part of Mao's name
35. Cobras
37. Extras, in music
38. Honey drink
40. Disen- tangled
42. To-do
43. Church listing
44. White clovers
46. To an extreme
47. Restore
48. Whirlpool
51. Hint
52. Dies ——
55. Ballet move- ment
57. Church service book
59. —— of strength
62. Cultivated
65. —— ahead (lead)
68. Cliff
69. Auditors
70. E Pluribus ——
71. Arizona sight
72. Prickly
76. Medical center
77. A rabbit
78. Atlas lines: Abbr.
80. Ghoul-like
82. John's problem, off and on
83. Newspaper pioneer
85. Rapidly
88. Settle down
90. Rory ——, Irish rebel
93. Spiny lily
95. "To —— truth"
96. Corroded
99. Appears suddenly
100. Obliging
101. —— punch
102. Lake, in Ireland
104. "To —— human"
106. Put into law
107. Biblical land: Var.
109. Bismarck
110. Speck
111. Soaks
113. Pronoun
116. Myrna
117. Prosecutors

Fit to Be Dyed
by Mary Murdoch

ACROSS

1. Meld
6. Variety bit
9. Black Sea arm
13. Signature of a playwright
19. Indian timber tree
20. Shout
21. Appoint
22. Record
23. Outer layer
25. Sea birds
28. Missile
29. —— de vie
31. Chemical prefix
32. Coin-tossing routine
33. Asparagus sprengeri
37. —— of dishes
38. Writings: Abbr.
39. Fare
40. Recent: Pref.
41. Adjective suffix
43. Corrupt
48. Brief biography
49. Méditerranée, for one
50. Coins
52. Girl's name
53. Cuts of meat
55. Witticism
56. Goodbyes in Roma
58. Droop
59. Time period
60. Mme. ——
63. Rats
65. Suffix for top or typ
66. Wine
67. Jane Fonda film
69. Mischievous: Sp.
70. Poet Walter et al.
72. Lozenge
73. Terry
75. Channel
76. Hairlike structure
77. Mountain passes
81. Observing
83. Landing vessels
84. Pales
86. Euryale, for instance
89. Italian man's name
91. Cassini
92. Mellow
93. Regards too highly
95. Theater tests
97. Springs
98. Cockney dwelling
99. Stew
101. Wife
102. Literary works
103. Carried on
105. Golf great
106. Ballet step
107. Sally ——
108. Trumpet call
110. Under warranty: Abbr.
111. Civic: Abbr.
112. Mass of ice
113. Sawlike: Prefix
116. Ohio city
118. English primrose
122. I.O.U. holders
127. Chemistry degree
128. Bear: Sp.
129. Moon valley
130. Smollett's spendthrift
133. Go back in
135. Indian
136. Exude
137. Be troubled
138. Sovereign's stand-in
139. Chair parts
140. Prong
141. Aves.
142. Horse sound

DOWN

1. Sayings
2. Holds forth
3. Air-tower gear
4. Drink flavoring
5. Goddess of healing
6. Debate
7. Sedan
8. Globe, for instance
9. Gun girl
10. Ibex
11. Melville novel
12. Kind of marble
13. Inhabited by gremlins
14. Salts
15. Comedian Laurel
16. Arizona tribe
17. Aleutian island
18. —— Indies
19. "Go —— Rover!"
24. Judith Anderson role
26. Ape
27. Docs
30. Fore's partner
34. Wagons-
35. Concerning
36. Kind of instrument
42. So ——
44. Sporting place
45. Flavoring
46. Missile places
47. "...could —— lean"
48. Common
49. Obligations
50. Unfeelingly
51. French coin
53. French school
54. Florida city
55. Dumas ——
57. Kind of wax
59. Spanish hero et al.
60. Carl Van
61. Renounced
62. Sooner
64. Asserts
66. Films
68. Certain discs
71. City official
74. Household gods
76. Litigant: Abbr.
78. Melodies
79. A Yokum
80. Scottish tools
82. Demantoid
84. Takes a trip
85. Business abbreviations
86. Burgess's boors
87. Immature seed
88. Varnish ingredient
90. Flower
94. Thine: Fr.
96. Some Arabians
97. Bills: Slang
100. Pilgrimage to Mecca
102. Simple's partner
104. Elation
106. Australian birds
107. Operetta composer
109. Headings: Fr.
111. Twice DCL
112. Certain noblemen: Abbr.
113. Fur worker
114. Give in
115. Passive
117. French pronoun
119. —— to eat
120. Carols
121. A Beatle
122. Accountants: Abbr.
123. Corded fabric
124. Of an age
125. Ten: Prefix
126. Kind of truck, for short
131. Fasten
132. Sat down
134. Pause fillers

What's That Again
by Elmer Toro

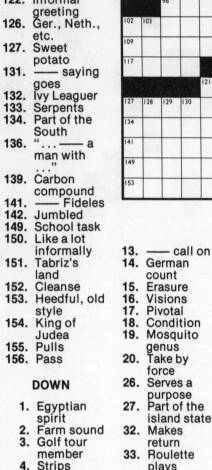

ACROSS

1. Sufficient
6. Fabric
10. Uriah's family
15. Carpenter's tool
21. Sacred text of Islam
22. Prepare
23. Available
24. Ham actor
25. Dance
28. Ill, in France
29. Director
30. "L' ——, c'est moi"
31. Disparages
33. Cheers
36. Tranquility, for one
38. Seven: Prefix
41. High peak
42. Direction: Abbr.
43. Tumult
46. Marienbad and others
47. Miss Street and others
49. By: Sp.
50. Attraction
52. A science: Abbr.
56. Swift's forte
57. Assuming airs
60. Garden workers
61. Go over with a dry mop
63. Born
64. Pensacola, for one: Abbr.
65. Eye parts
66. Kind of novel: Abbr.
67. Jumble
72. Boxing champ of the '20s
73. Crew chiefs, for short
75. Be in the red
76. Rialto sign
77. Hitchcock movie
80. Hard wood
81. In opposition
85. Ralph
88. Two or more eras
89. Tools for cutting holes
91. Word of disgust
93. Fleming
94. Certain beans: Var.
96. Entice
97. Mischief
101. A kind of stick
102. Quemoy's neighbor
104. Crag
105. Muslim saint
106. Maltreats
109. Nautical term
110. Deceit
115. Mythical darkness
117. Set of three
118. Stadium call
119. Royal initials
120. Actress Judge
121. Hesitates
122. Informal greeting
126. Ger., Neth., etc.
127. Sweet potato
131. —— saying goes
132. Ivy Leaguer
133. Serpents
134. Part of the South
136. "... —— a man with ..."
139. Carbon compound
141. —— Fideles
142. Jumbled
149. School task
150. Like a lot informally
151. Tabriz's land
152. Cleanse
153. Heedful, old style
154. King of Judea
155. Pulls
156. Pass

DOWN

1. Egyptian spirit
2. Farm sound
3. Golf tour member
4. Strips
5. Noun suffix
6. Black widow
7. St. Pierre, for one
8. Shoe part
9. Sea speed unit
10. More piquant
11. Ref. book
12. An anesthetic: Abbr.
13. —— call on
14. German count
15. Erasure
16. Visions
17. Pivotal
18. Condition
19. Mosquito genus
20. Take by force
26. Serves a purpose
27. Part of the island state
32. Makes return
33. Roulette plays
34. Lend ——
35. Every which way
37. Xanadu's river
39. Map
40. Printing error, for short
43. Wildly
44. ——-hoo
45. Attract
46. Bristles
48. Put the ——
(shut)
51. Metallic sound
52. Desire strongly
53. Willies
54. Period of history
55. Writings: Abbr.
58. Letter
59. Slangy answers
60. Confusedly
62. Biblical pronouns
68. Have
69. Army unit: Abbr.
70. Ganymede, for one
71. Female rabbit
72. Muffin
73. Plant study: Abbr.
74. Crew member
77. Uncle ——
78. Tibetan animal
79. Cricket sides
82. Person
83. Sea eagle
84. Korean soldier
86. Yutang
87. "Mighty —— a rose ..."
90. Korean port
92. Yarn measure
95. Black Bird
97. Derisive cries
98. Curved lines
99. Godly: It.
100. "—— and Mehitabel"
102. Rug
103. Fortas
104. "Arms and ——"
107. Fancywork
108. Dawn
111. Expressions of disgust
112. Chimney dirt
113. Bean of India
114. Pump
116. Sunday talks: Abbr.
118. Tolerant
121. Creator of Shangri-La
123. Passed, as time
124. Greek district
125. Fatty acids
127. City in Florida
128. Youngest son
129. Take —— (pause)
130. Moon crater
131. In reserve
133. Exhausted
135. Exclamation of surprise
137. Do a newsroom job
138. Learner
140. Monster
143. British oath
144. 12 dozen: Abbr.
145. Handle rudely
146. A Spanish queen
147. Medal: Abbr.
148. Again

Variety Package

by Peter E. Price

ACROSS

1. Children's game
11. Priest's vestment
14. "Pease porridge ——..."
20. Circumspect monkey
21. Aces
23. Washrooms of a sort: Var.
24. Anybody's guess
25. Dutch pottery
26. Shelley's elegy for Keats
28. Wire: Abbr.
29. Mustard, laughing, etc.
30. Tartu's river
31. High: Music
33. Word for bad liquor
35. —— bad example
37. Henry and Jane
39. "Mona Lisa," et al.
41. Capital of Spain under Moors
46. Certain starlets
48. —— and ahed
49. Mobile home
50. Song of French Revolution
51. Make a move
54. Red Sea land
56. Wroclaw's river
57. Champion filly, 1957-8
58. Calliope et al.
59. Indian tourist attraction
61. Pro ——
62. Repair
63. —— Douglas, novelist
65. Rebel
66. —— standstill
67. Chaney
68. Scared out
70. Kind of poet
72. Chinese river
74. Teutonic god
75. Tried
77. Famed New York boss
79. Smallest state capital
82. Before Sept.
83. Western group: Abbr.
84. Alias the Cowardly Lion
86. Lap robe
87. Railroad network: Abbr.
88. Gullet
91. Society founded in 1776
94. Ness and others
96. Honeycombs: Lat.
97. Type size
98. Cafe
99. It —— much to ask
100. W.H. —— poet
101. Where the wise old owl sat
103. Clock sounds
105. Pension plan of the '30s
107. Prudent: It.
108. Tomb of the
111. N.Y. lake
112. Invitation P.S.
114. Korean city
115. Brave talk
116. Evergreen
117. Put-ons
121. Pronoun
123. Testing devices
125. Hebrew measures
127. Musical based on "Shrew"
130. Child's behavior at times
132. Yore
133. Alms: Lat.
134. Opera by Verdi
135. Music to torero's ears
136. Radio transmitter

DOWN

1. Daddy long-legs genus
2. Egg, in Paris
3. City in S. Calif.
4. Shifted: Abbr.
5. —— a time
6. Detroit name
7. Thighbones
8. Chekhov's first play
9. Formal award
10. The sign, to a Spaniard
11. Nootka Indian
12. Booty
13. Monday ailment
14. Somewhat: Suffix
15. Falls for a married woman
16. King of Siam's friend
17. Jet housings
18. Andaman people
19. Birthplace of Anacreon
22. Selective philosophy
23. Tom Collins without the kick
25. Fiscal problem
27. Unspecified quantity
32. Rival of Tulane
34. Closet bar
36. Jewish scriptures
38. Member of F.D.R. Cabinet
39. Medals
40. Neighbor of la.
42. Fashion name
43. Card game
44. French headgear
45. Famous mountain
47. French waters
52. Author of "The Caretakers"
53. Northern capital
55. Town in N.W. France
58. Big name in vases
59. Mock orange
60. God of the winds
62. Caress
64. At a loss, financially
67. New Guinea port
68. Missouri mountains
69. Isn't it, Shakespeare style
71. Thermometer abbreviation
72. Book by Sammy Davis
73. Russian composer
76. Reimburses
77. Venetian fishing boats
78. Woman, in Hawaii
80. Ptomaines found in meat
81. Adjective suffixes
85. Part of a box score
87. Scat!
88. Ogled
89. Persons exacting retribution
90. Casements
92. Injunctions
93. Aleutian isl.
95. Small beds
96. Brouhaha
99. Kind of triangle: Var.
100. Quinn and Newley
102. Scullers
104. Jewish delicacies
106. Suffix for polli
109. Onetime N.Y. greeter Grover ——
110. Voided
113. Dun-colored: Prefix
115. —— -les-Bains, France
117. Terrier
118. Yesterday: Fr.
119. Org.'s cousin
120. Russian river
122. Latin abbr.
124. Book by E.E. Cummings
126. Handwriting on the wall
128. Silkworm
129. Prior to
131. Slum area need: Abbr.

Words to the Wise

by A.J. Santora

ACROSS

1. Assemble
5. Victor's due
9. Hebrew letter
13. Dennis of tennis
20. Indigo
21. Prefix with distant
22. Stevenson's retreat
23. Factor
24. Taro
25. Discovers
27. Limits
28. Benét play, with "The"
31. Lead a horse
32. Nagy of Hungary
33. Strange
34. Alert
35. Type of ink
37. Bizarre
39. Rebozo
44. Hosp. people
45. Goad
47. Parts of ski lifts
49. Ref. book
51. Square
52. Arthur of tennis
54. Silvery salmon
56. Flabella
58. Management's concern
60. Rent
62. With 79 Across, an old "Laugh In" phrase
64. Misuses the thermostat
66. Gems
69. Hong Kong or Asian
70. Direction
71. Split
72. West Indian music
74. Spelling ____
75. Farm tool inventor
76. ____ disant
79. See 62 Across
85. Map abbreviation
86. Hunter of the sky
87. Oahu town
88. Spiteful ones: Colloq.
89. Payment
91. ____ Anne

92. College at Cedar Rapids
94. Fat
95. Dredging bucket
98. Nuclear experiments
100. Predatory fish
101. Young hare
102. Nobleman
104. Urban problem
106. ____ pinch of salt
110. Sobeit
111. Symington, familiarly
113. Brisk
115. Gulpers
117. Fleming
118. Pari ____ (equally)
120. Writing fluid: Fr.
122. Approaches
124. Style of painting
126. Hilum
128. Yastrzemski
129. Comedians of a sort
131. Forgotten names are left to them, said Preston

137. Alpaca's cousin
138. Flattened: Sl.
139. Without: Fr.
141. Ring-shaped
142. Eared seal
143. Prefix with plasm
144. N. Z. pine
145. Roof style
146. Dogs, for short
147. "____ in the course of ..."
148. Italian family

DOWN

1. West
2. Ups ____
3. Lateral air-flow
4. Czech neighbor
5. Mesta
6. Zoo's counterpart
7. Sally ____
8. Flubbed
9. Chili con ____
10. To me: Fr.
11. Model
12. Meat dish

13. Viewpoint
14. Excuse
15. Glasses
16. Struck
17. Head, in Paris
18. Unique person
19. P.M. times
22. Beetle gem
26. Confess
29. Adherents: Abbr.
30. "If I ____ king"
31. Scarlett's estate
36. Rock
37. Speak
38. Initials on a skivvy
40. Despised
41. Song
42. Departed
43. Falls back
46. L.A. time
48. ____ of fish
50. Procession
53. Glen ____, Ill.
55. Costello
57. "____ the rose"
59. Pronoun
61. Detect
63. Sharp
65. Panorama

66. Eye: Prefix
67. Dad
68. Got down
69. Crossword puzzle standby
73. Placates
74. Savarin
75. The double helix
76. Skated
77. Fashion first name
78. Paris suburb
80. Coin of Iran
81. Kitty of novel
82. Bide ____
83. California wine area
84. Order of frogs
89. Signs
90. Guard unit: Abbr.
91. European river: Fr. sp.
92. Football player: Abbr.
93. Willow
95. Applaud
96. Late golf pro
97. Sts.
99. Lively music

100. Take form
103. Continent: Abbr.
105. Eating pal
107. Graphs
108. Chickens out
109. Termites
112. Preposition
114. Flashy: Informal
116. Call for cattle
119. College in East Orange, N.J.
121. Drive-in girl
123. Fully renovated
125. Verse
127. Movie award
128. Shades of brown
130. Undealt cards
131. Panama Indian
132. ____ of Cutch
133. Burden
134. ____ a turn
135. Stroller
136. Engrave
137. Group of whales
140. Prosecute

Point of View by William Lutwiniak

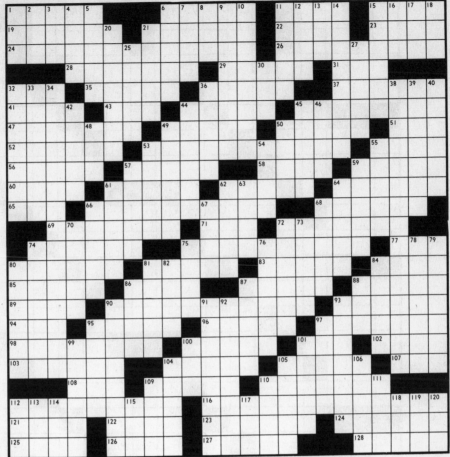

ACROSS

1. Flavorful seed
6. Turkish V.I.P.
11. Potter's adjunct
15. Hymenopteron
19. Oil color vehicle
21. Hearing defect of sorts
22. Federal org.
23. Corn lily
24. Time of the week
26. They know everything
28. Musical passages
29. Give-and-take affairs
31. Teachers' org.
32. Stomach
35. Peerage members
36. Honshu volcano
37. Layers
41. Chemical endings
43. Family members
44. Boors
45. Like some tomatoes
47. Be social
49. Halloween costume
50. Irish darling
51. Pre-——
52. Outdoor people
53. With 24 Across, a know-it-all
55. Entr'——
56. Proxy
57. Malayan sirs
58. Barnyard sound
59. Different
60. Football play
61. Garment
62. Eased off
64. Scuba fishing gear
65. Depressing
66. Words from a "friend"
68. Mother of Achilles
69. European bison
71. Numerical prefix
72. Wood finisher
74. Accumulating
75. Certain

remarks
77. Motorist's need
80. Fine wool
81. Name in Broadway fame
83. Embellish
84. Dream: Fr.
85. Kind of verb: Abbr.
86. By hand: Prefix
87. Irish spade
88. French painter
89. Incursion
90. Bridge-table encores
93. Go back
94. G.I. address
95. Very: Music
96. Disseminates, as tales
97. Distinct
98. Desert rodent
100. Takes five
101. Ruler: Abbr.
102. Wise
103. Early ascetic
104. Contradict
105. Hussar's gear
107. Had charge

108. Object
109. Valentine figure
110. Salty one
112. It's always 20-20
116. Unerring appraisals
121. By word
122. Cover fully
123. Cutlery
124. Young eels
125. Terrier
126. Weakens
127. Longhorn
128. Servicewomen

DOWN

1. Sand: Prefix
2. Modern: Prefix
3. Auto system: Abbr.
4. Caesar et al.
5. Lift up
6. Reels: Scot.
7. Harding et al.
8. Six in Italy
9. Distributes
10. Moot
11. Ollie's friend
12. Oxford's river

13. Place for books: Abbr.
14. Soft muslin
15. Sorceror
16. Fireman's gear
17. Title
18. Family members
20. Ill-starred lover
21. Works hard
25. Corday's victim
27. Grand ——
30. German river
32. Accidents
33. Leeward island
34. Part-timers
36. Then: Fr.
38. Fighter of a kind
39. Lacks stability
40. Math aces
42. Disbursed
44. Crude shelter
45. Mark
46. Fasten
48. Scrap for Fido
49. Protects
50. Rose's love

53. Coverlet
54. Newspaper part, for short
55. Tete-——
57. Leather strip
59. Certain sports tourneys
61. Office help
62. Engraving tool
63. —— were
64. Leveling wedges
66. "Of thee ——"
67. Other: Sp.
68. Cup: Fr.
70. Venerably traditional
72. Skedaddles
73. French exclamation
74. Ponchos
75. Fish bait
76. Unproductive ones
78. Mean
79. Orderly
80. Delusion
81. Social class
82. Knowledgeable
84. Ecstatic reviews

86. Girl's name
87. Condition
88. Cyclotron abbreviation
90. Art of disputation
91. Certain monuments
92. Not migratory
93. Income
95. Some skirts
97. Ferber novel
99. Parish official
100. Congressman: Abbr.
101. Carnelians
104. Tag ends
105. More reasoned
106. Fishing gear
109. Fellow
110. Action
111. Initials on a card
112. Exclamations
113. Nettle
114. Vote against
115. Area of India
117. French co.
118. Multitude
119. Misdo
120. Draft initials

Passing the Word

by Cornelia Warriner

ACROSS

1. Hanger-on
5. Rascal
10. Metal beam
14. Hobo's vegetable
18. Tennis star
19. Light craft
20. Uncanny
21. Chicago name
22. TV fare of sorts
25. Noted jockey
26. Nautical chain
27. Yew
28. Roundup gear
29. Prepares to swim the Channel
30. Sea birds
31. French psychologist
32. Short
33. Baldwins
36. Dancer Pauline
37. Workmanship
41. Restrain
42. Computer workers
44. Form of Rachel
45. Lips
46. Silk, in Paris
47. River to the Seine
48. Sea-story writer
49. Elec. unit
50. Press items
54. Ship
55. Is worthwhile
57. Like a child's nose
58. Hair tints
59. Anon
60. Eye cell parts
61. Once, in a prescription
62. Slender probe
64. Emphatic words
65. Some news items
68. Shrew and others
69. Brinkley, Wallace et al.
71. Spinner
72. Solar deity
73. Prefix for an antiseptic
74. Former diva
75. Places: Lat.

76. Three-way joint
77. Without words
81. Sea off Australia
82. "—— its martyrs"
84. And —— grow on
85. Scuffle
86. Rabbit
87. Ship parts
88. Positive
89. British party
92. Add
93. Both: Prefix
94. Old French coin
97. Rig out
98. Cramped quarters
101. Sausage
102. Roman road
103. Fiber for rugs
104. Baseball team
105. Soil

106. Disorder
107. Heat, as milk
108. Stepped

DOWN
1. Tense
2. Catch sight of
3. Loafer
4. Lacrosse team
5. Mocks
6. Concerns
7. Handle: Fr.
8. Family member
9. Shedding
10. Mosaic piece
11. Animal
12. Jason's ship
13. Ham on ——
14. Biblical words
15. Criticizes: Colloq.
16. Muslim tongue
17. Ocean, to poets

21. Egyptian god
23. Infection for short
24. Sounder
29. Way out: Fr.
30. Trees
31. One kind of fan
32. A garnish
33. Catch ——
34. Some TV time
35. Publicity agent of yore
36. Name for Santa
37. Concord
38. U.N. workers
39. Indian title
40. Leap and light
42. T.V.A. output
43. A.M.'s to poets
46. Divide
48. Entertained

50. Memos
51. Notched: Bot.
52. Roman wars, 264-146 B.C.
53. Burdens: Lat.
54. Delineates
56. Certain bucket
58. Brings up
60. Punctuation mark
61. Location
62. Marine ray
63. Fire ——
64. River nymphs of Greek myth
65. Mouth: Prefix
66. Kind of train
67. Heavy stake
69. Not up ——
70. Roasting rods
73. The men —— life
75. Mislay

77. Intrude suddenly
78. Wavers
79. Golfing words
80. Old capital of Egypt
81. Item for a whatnot
83. Orchestra man
85. Took a bath
87. Shoe parts
88. —— a rat
89. Obscene
90. Water: Prefix
91. Famous duelist
92. Mal de ——
93. Theater org.
94. Recipe word
95. Words of disbelief
96. Kind of car
98. Dickens boy
99. Vibrate: Abbr.
100. Can. province

Stepquote

by Eugene T. Maleska

ACROSS

1. Start of an eleven-word quote descending in stairstep fashion to 143 Across
7. Misfit of W.W. II
14. Lorraine's partner
20. White's "—— from the Fortieth Floor"
21. Interstices
22. Peter made three
24. Encore for boxers
25. Argentine seaport
26. Stepquote source
27. Words of confidence
28. What debeo means
30. Indian weight
31. Tam-tam
32. Prefix for gram or logue
33. Boone
34. Type of bigot
36. False
38. Two cups
39. Sheep
41. Stepquote part
44. Style name
45. Flood and spring
46. Flee
48. Vaughan et al.
50. TV cabinets
52. Barkley
54. Write a music score
56. Paris subway
57. Lone
61. Heel over
63. Terminal
66. Cap-——
67. Funny fellows
69. Isle of the oracle
71. Cognition
73. Tennis terms
74. Theater section
75. Scattering
77. Moist
78. Nobel product
79. Goes out on a limb
81. Indiana Indians
82. No longer new
84. Emergency care
85. Where Zeno taught
87. Hoover Dam's lake
88. Calm
90. Not for all the —— China
91. Staggers
92. Ye —— tea shoppe
93. Estimate
95. See 57 Across
97. Summoned back
99. For —— sake!
101. Mend the oxfords
103. Ruined city in Iran
104. Fish spears
107. Logomachy
109. Be frugal
113. The mating game
114. Layer
116. Stepquote part
118. Levant or Hammerstein
119. Zola's "Le ——" (1888)
120. Military lodging
122. With the result
124. —— pro nobis
125. St. Pierre
126. Buffoon
127. Yemeni
130. Sediment
131. Struck
132. Citizens of Valletta
134. Bohemian composer
136. Flaccid
138. Stepquote author
139. Baby hare
140. Expanded
141. "Thanatopsis" poet
142. Cuban province
143. End of Stepquote

DOWN

1. Novel by R.P. Warren (1959)
2. Sanguineous
3. Author Hunter
4. Mass. campus
5. Spore clusters of rust fungi
6. Stepquote part
7. Willy Loman, for one
8. Coach Parseghian
9. Gov't. branch
10. Concert rendition
11. Babylonian deity
12. —— mouse game
13. Large parrot
14. Recessed
15. Sierra ——
16. Close-fitting
17. Publicize
18. Voltaire hero
19. Malbin, Stritch, etc.
20. Camera support
23. Jalousie
29. Comes in first
31. Make neat
34. Convened again
35. Old card games
37. Twitch
38. Guided
40. Blues
42. Judo exercises
43. Stepquote part
45. Body part
47. Brilliant gray
49. See 38 Down
51. Goad
53. A —— (presumptive)
55. Sniggler
57. Break of continuity
58. Bounding main
59. Scatters trash
60. Dieter's dish
62. Not at all
64. "Not so deep —— ..."
65. Citrus drink
68. Makes taut
70. Carrie or Kenny
72. Dug
75. Type of glass
76. Uganda group: Var.
80. Elevator's neighbor
83. Scorn
84. Olivia's clown
86. Spore sac
87. Teeth
89. Obligations
91. Passes on
94. Opinion
96. Tennis strokes
98. Neckcloth
100. Fence stairs
102. Bleach
104. "Behold —— of God
..."
105. Convivial one
106. Salt: Fr.
108. This, in Spain
110. "—— bury Caesar..."
111. Seaman
112. Babbled
113. Malfeasant's act
115. Fruit-juice gadget
117. Stepquote part
120. Wisent
121. "Three Coins" fountain
123. Savory jelly
126. Pueblo site
128. Fit to ——
129. Bossy's home
131. Skiddoo
133. Essay
134. Road sign
135. Trampoline
137. Bantu language

Miscellany

by Jack Luzzatto

ACROSS

1. Spotting systems
7. Certain storage places
14. Pause in verse: Var.
20. Vinegary
21. Drowsing
22. Legal claimant
23. Bee's goal
24. Swimmer
25. Way out
26. Verse
27. Tries the bait
29. Tin Pan Alley girl
31. Used up
32. Initial score
34. Especially gifted one
36. Temple, old style
37. Small town
38. Paint tester
39. Fattened steer
40. Martinique volcano
42. Causerie
43. Sacred mountain in Szechwan
45. Merchant to an army
47. Desert hazard
49. Cicero topic
53. Pushes on
54. Closes the gap
55. Rope-ladder rungs
57. Shopping centers
58. Savory
59. Sets a tempo
60. Hymenopter
61. People for
62. Clairvoyance
64. Chaser for tequila
65. Large lizard
66. Less
67. Silas Marner's golden girl
68. Worthwhile quality
69. Regions
71. Of an Eastern people
72. Capital of Albania: Var.
73. Artificial
74. Harness ring
76. Turned into
77. Name for a field dog
79. Awry
80. Sublease
81. Vilify
84. Get along well
86. —— noire
87. Sum, ——, fui
91. Newsprint plants
93. John 1:1-14 as part of a mass
95. Shooting match: Fr.
96. Tropical sunhat
97. Small-horse drivers
98. Clear
99. Draw forth
101. Iatric
103. Bring into accord
105. Opening
106. Cut off
107. Patcher
108. Wobble
109. Braced for shock
110. Virulent ones

DOWN

1. Decamped
2. Sin of sloth
3. Decree in Scotland
4. Lawyer: Abbr.
5. Laughing
6. Jots down
7. Caliber
8. Kind of computer
9. Ranked
10. Dolorous word
11. Achieve
12. Abrasives
13. Try
14. Do housework
15. Teatime at sea
16. Discourse: Abbr.
17. Discomfort
18. Seaport on the Don
19. Leblanc thief Lupin
28. Not so gay
30. Classic roué
33. Singing groups
34. Gains altitude
35. Swiss miss
38. Grilling
41. Right-angle extensions
42. Linked set
44. Religious music
45. More chic
46. Hullabaloos
47. Lukewarmness
48. Lamentable
50. Word switch
51. Real
52. Fourth ——
53. Ascribe
54. Most precise
56. Athletic aftermath
58. In stitches
59. Songbird
62. Usurp
63. Binge
64. Ventilates
66. Image of eternity
68. Cheese fanciers
70. Small civet
71. Impels
72. Signal one's punches
75. Most be-times
76. Davis
78. Jackpot starter
80. Rebounded
81. Best, as a pupil
82. Receiver of goods
83. Rebel
85. A thanedom for Macbeth
86. District in Yugoslavia
88. Neat
89. Fisherman
90. Churchmen
92. Measurer
93. Union unit
94. Port of old Rome
97. Heap
100. Small boat
102. Female hare
104. Oriental New Year

Literal World
by Anthony Morse

17

ACROSS

1. Anaconda's relative
6. Prankster
11. Spectral type in the sky
16. City near Bombay
21. Type of architecture
22. Yellowish-red color
23. High spot
24. Ration
25. Relatives in Haarlem
27. Poilus march off
29. Stub ——
30. Carol
31. Candy
33. Father of Ajax
34. Row
35. African antelopes
36. Lancelot's uncle
37. Satellites
41. Modern name for Lutetia
42. Without pity
43. Exclamation
47. Doctrinal rejection
48. Rascals in Havana
50. Court decree
51. Fads
52. Venetian feature
53. Bad
54. Buck
55. Matured
56. Suffix for some acids
57. Aquatic mammal
61. Relative of 1 Across
62. Star
63. A locale in "My Fair Lady"
65. Whole
66. Rests upon
68. "...the end is not ——"
69. Weapon for a soldado
73. World area
74. Ancient road
76. Man: Latin
77. Specially-shaped clock
78. Scottish resort
80. Compos mentis
82. Young man got mad
88. Drink
91. Invention
93. Dutch cupboard
94. Auriculate
95. Choler
96. —— Roy
97. Establishes
100. Heel over
101. Anti, out west
102. —— la Cité
104. Period
105. "To —— human"
106. Celestial fluid
107. Entreat
108. Bahians off the beam
111. Pin used in ceramics
112. Former Chief Justice
113. Prune
114. Certain paintings
115. Supports
116. Carriage
117. Doesn't exist
118. Old Brazilian money
119. Navy men
123. More depressed
124. English poet
125. Nautical word
129. Cockneys take a close look
131. Gossips in Lampang
134. Shepherd in "As You Like It"
135. Tarzan's rope
136. Talk-show host
137. Thin mortar
138. Filch: Slang
139. Joined
140. Ancient tomb
141. Islamic spirit

DOWN

1. Opera girl
2. Set-to
3. Preposition
4. Trio of rhyme
5. Berliner's alas
6. Craft
7. Result of high-pressure living
8. A kind of road
9. Japanese apricot
10. Rural poem
11. Disreputable
12. Feudal people
13. Card
14. River to the Rhone
15. College officials
16. Cloys
17. Tree genus
18. Spatial infinity
19. New: Prefix
20. Egyptian disk
26. Concord
28. Drove
32. Neat as
34. Heroine of 1891 novel
35. French smoker's need
36. Circus purchase
37. Full of sayings
38. Three miles
39. Squawk from Peron
40. Requirement
41. Penal
42. Tutoring
43. Charlemagne's domain: Abbr.
44. Dark periods in Riyadh
45. Lead-part players
46. Finally
48. Religious law
49. Norse goddess
50. Mime
52. Early associate of Caesar
57. Ale server
58. Arabs
59. Common contraction
60. Bristly
63. Enzyme suffix
64. Wrench
65. 1952 Pulitzer play with "The"
67. Shoe material: Abbr.
70. Bro's opposite
71. O.K.
72. Ace ——
75. Refreshment
79. River bottom
80. Director's guide
81. Swiss pine
83. Cattle genus
84. Meantime
85. Headland
86. Eastern women
87. Bits
89. Baltimore man
90. Styles
92. Even
98. Ancient Syria
99. Siberian river
100. Vial
101. Feigns
103. Grammar case: Abbr.
105. Approves
106. Notes
108. Without restraint
109. Covered in a way
110. Moon figure
111. Evaporates
113. Spanish numeral
115. Early U.S. homes
116. Penalty, in France
117. Form of Helen
118. A Montague
119. Less than mins.
120. Omar word
121. Old Roman fields
122. Radar dot
123. Bill
124. Gait
125. Israeli port
126. Capital of Aisne
127. Case
128. Italian family
130. Godly: It.
132. Rascal
133. Embryonic fowl

Music Lesson

by John Owens

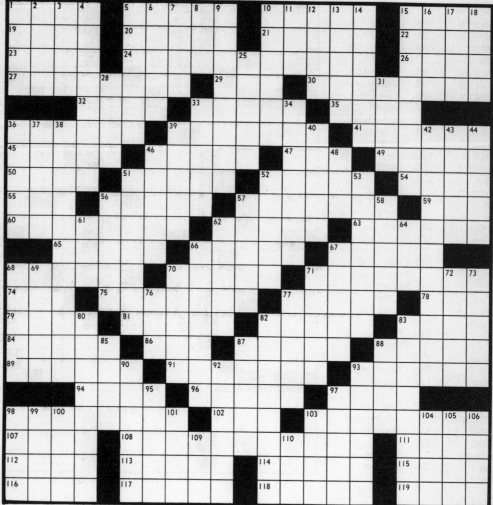

ACROSS

1. Gil ——
5. Stunted tree
10. Doze
15. Some radio men
19. Hindu scale
20. Record player: Abbr.
21. Anathema
22. Thanks ——
23. Borodin hero
24. Beethoven Quartets Opus 59
26. Part of N.B.
27. Musical quality
29. A kind of ear
30. Quadrangle
32. Prohibits
33. Kind of pie
35. Reddish brown
36. Song: Ger.
39. Following
41. Decoration on metal
45. Imitating
46. Disease germ
47. Breach
49. Dehydrated
50. Reward, old style
51. Spanish cleric
52. Noted columnist
54. Flying prefix
55. Plead
56. Passageway
57. "Turn of the Screw" composer
59. —— jour
60. Evil Jewish spirit
62. Do a grammar chore
63. Amen
65. Uneven
66. Pentateuch
67. Passengers
68. Monks
70. Indian soldier
71. Choral works
74. —— Alamos
75. Danish composer (1865-1931)
77. —— organ
78. Irving character
79. French opera section
81. Soot marks
82. Lowland: Scot.
83. Sheath
84. Perfume
86. Paleolithic, for one
87. French painter
88. Greenland base
89. U.S. composer
91. Composer of symphonic poems
93. Rang a bell
94. Lawyers: Abbr.
96. Tidal flood
97. Connery
98. Italian opera, with "La"
102. Large bird
103. One kind of partner
107. —— soit ...
108. Baroque forms of composition
111. College course: Abbr.
112. Greek letters
113. U.S. emblem
114. Stale
115. Bristle
116. System: Abbr.
117. Taters
118. Misplayed
119. Waste allowance

DOWN

1. Small herring
2. Como
3. Greek contest
4. Spanish dance
5. Schumann's first symphony
6. Talks
7. Optimistic
8. One: It.
9. Small shop
10. Wall bracket
11. Former Broadway play
12. Formerly, old style
13. Glacial ridge
14. TV place
15. Carmen specialty
16. Shake ——
17. Prefix for gram or lith
18. British gun
25. Without
28. Eng. or Lat.
31. Police activity
33. Lehar's widow
34. Title of six Bach suites
36. Viola da
37. Swords
38. Composer of "Ozark Set"
39. Teams
40. Experience
42. Liszt opus
43. Vive ——
44. Tooth: Prefix
46. Worth
48. Kitty
51. South African composer
52. Finery
53. Heavily: Music
56. Ornament
57. Nobleman
58. Direction
61. —— pro nobis
62. Gregory et al.
64. Miss Lillie
66. Having left a will
67. Opera
68. Gordon of the comics
69. Composer of the "Dybbuk"
70. Legatos
71. Centers
72. Passageway
73. Tempo
76. Uncle: Dialect
77. Pastor's home
80. Throw into ecstasy
82. Old French dance
83. Violin part
85. S.A. monkey
87. Myopic cartoon Mister
88. —— she blows!
90. Conditions
92. Egyptian king
93. Stopped
95. Subway fixture
97. Outpouring
98. Pronoun
99. Routine
100. Med. course
101. Pointed: Fr.
103. Recipe word
104. Cooler
105. Half or quarter, for instance
106. Pest
109. King Cole
110. Timetable abbreviation

Space Madness

by Eileen Bush

ACROSS

1. Early astronaut program
7. Particular: Abbr.
11. Truman's birthplace
16. Universe: Prefix
21. One of a meteor swarm
22. Cinema, in Europe
23. —— in arms
24. Hollywood name
25. Suffers attrition
26. Name of a planet's transit, perhaps
28. Chic
29. Forty ——
30. Rejects
31. Old and New
33. Kind of sign
34. Silly
35. Paw: Fr.
37. Like a julep
38. "The groves were God's first ——"
40. Spells
41. Numerical prefix
42. —— Magnon
44. Light ——
45. Drilled
46. Look of sorts
47. Chinese name
50. Round figure
52. Shore birds
53. Fighter planes
55. Conductor's word
56. River to the Colorado
57. Inform
58. Soviet moon rocket
59. Warm glow
60. Docking
63. Early dulcimer
64. Band, in heraldry
65. Humid
66. Art works
67. Fan
68. Seep
69. Artist's wear
71. —— d'oeuvre
72. Oct. 31 wear
76. Juncture
77. Ruth's husband
78. U.S. satellite
82. Narcotic
83. Dive, astronaut style
86. Upper space
87. Stroke on a letter
88. Twofold
89. Pronoun
90. Rise
91. Pendants on watch chains
93. Water bird
95. Absent
96. Desire
97. Reddish color
98. Employes
99. Part of N.B.
100. "To —— With Love"
101. Descended
102. Face for 72 Across
103. Organ stop
105. Kiel or Suez
107. Legal plea
108. Shopping areas
109. Color
112. Computing machine
114. Substantial
116. Overeats
117. Illinois city
118. Lunar blues, so to speak
120. Catch one's ——
121. Alpine peak
122. Mountain chain
123. Attracted
124. Kind of bean soup
125. A Churchill
126. Seed coating
127. Indian weights
128. Direction on a ship

DOWN

1. Early astronaut
2. Uncanny
3. Like lunar living?
4. Oily hydrocarbon
5. Deny: Fr.
6. Libidos
7. Master of a vessel
8. G.I.-locker photos
9. Access
10. Bathos: Slang
11. Wash basin: Abbr.
12. Backed in a way
13. Certain art works
14. Malign
15. Balance
16. Humor for serious astronauts
17. Former Philippine President
18. Meager
19. Borgnine role
20. Scraps
27. Ad astra per ——
30. Chef's creation
32. Mohammedan noble
34. Moonship's forte
36. Implements
39. Perfume ingredient
40. Greek goddesses
41. U.S.
42. Poke fun at
43. 100 kopecks
45. Forward
46. Maid
47. Helden- ——
48. Fence passage
49. Glacial ridge
51. That: Ger.
52. Retrogress
53. Under: Fr.
54. Burlap fiber
56. Part of a chromosome
57. U.S. President
60. Level
61. Goes like a spaceship
62. London's Old ——
63. French preposition
65. Type of roof
67. Fictional detective
68. Sign on astronaut's door
69. Convince: Colloq.
70. Pasture sound
71. Intimidates
72. TV star Bill
73. —— citato
74. Tempter of Ulysses
75. Part of a comet
76. Hot Springs et al.
77. Biography word
78. Do art work
79. Moon eruption, perhaps
80. Frenchman's name
81. Fraternal group
83. Fat
84. Host
85. Music pieces
86. Colorado park
88. Do housework
90. Top-notchers: Colloq.
92. Old pen
93. Half: Ger.
94. Navy man
95. Form of Helen
98. Snood
99. U.S. painter
101. Seaport of Italy
102. Inundates
103. One who sponges
104. Aid to success
105. Type of lily
106. Church area
107. In harmony
108. Watered silk
110. Type of nonsense
111. Pale
112. Hacks
113. Common Latin verb
115. Tote board listings
116. Mardi ——
119. Bible book: Abbr.
120. Win —— mile

Birth of a Nation
by Bert Beaman

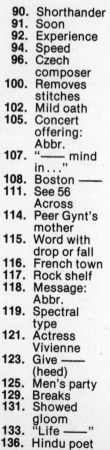

ACROSS

1. Varnish ingredient
6. Basket fiber
11. U.S. author
16. Time and —
21. Home
22. Godunov
23. Architecture style
24. —— Khali (Arabian desert)
25. "...becomes —— dissolve..." (from 111 Across)
29. Certain Alaskans: Abbr.
30. Rely on
31. Town in Maine
32. —— Forge
33. —— light
35. Oilskin hat
37. Asian civet
39. Forward
40. Rips
42. Store
44. Rage
46. Stationery item: Abbr.
48. Shakespearean character
50. Chemical suffixes
52. Bovary
53. Kind of dirt
56. With 111 Across, a document
59. "...us beyond —— tried..."
61. Networks
62. Resting
63. Asian river
65. Items on pirate flags
66. W.W. II vessels
68. Action: Suffix
70. Range
73. Golfer's concerns
74. Fat: Prefix
76. Smorgasbord items
79. Fabric finish
80. Being: Lat.
81. "—— Governments are instituted ..."
87. Make over
88. Laugh: Fr.
89. Flying prefix
90. Shorthander
91. Soon
92. Experience
94. Speed
96. Czech composer
100. Removes stitches
102. Mild oath
105. Concert offering: Abbr.
107. "—— mind in..."
108. Boston ——
111. See 56 Across
114. Peer Gynt's mother
115. Word with drop or fall
116. French town
117. Rock shelf
118. Message: Abbr.
119. Spectral type
121. Actress Vivienne
123. Give —— (heed)
125. Men's party
129. Breaks
131. Showed gloom
133. "Life ——"
136. Hindu poet
138. Kind of ion: Suffix
140. "—— the West Wind"
142. River to the Rhine
143. "Our Lives, —— Honor"
147. Spaces
148. Alla —— in music
149. Remoulade
150. Reach
151. Layers
152. Beasts
153. —— Testament: Ger.
154. Gray

DOWN

1. Sticks
2. Portly
3. President's stratagem
4. —— Fideles
5. French article
6. Construction piece
7. Spore cluster
8. Carpenters' gauges
9. Erect
10. Inner: Prefix
11. Scent
12. Revere
13. Scenes of action
14. Counterstrokes
15. King conqueror
16. Harp: It.
17. Prepares peas
18. Poplar
19. Approach midnight
20. A signer of 56 Across
26. Spatial
27. Balkan state
28. Subdued
34. Attack
36. Came down
38. Certain
41. Stage direction
43. British cavalry force: Abbr.
45. Cover
46. Common French verb
47. Pacific islands: Abbr.
49. Union members
51. Close
53. Kosciuszko, for one
54. Most qualified
55. Words of assent
57. Phone sounds
58. Au revoir
60. Large fowl of West
64. Track event
67. One at a stadium mike
69. Antitoxins
71. Deform
72. Combine with: Suffix
75. Global area
77. Richard Henry ——
78. Rope part: Abbr.
81. Shock
82. Certain rinses
83. With one's back to: Fr.
84. Whale
85. Accumulate
86. Normans, for example
93. Psychiatrist's problems
95. Paid: Slang
97. Tracked down
98. Noun ending
99. Ship part
101. Admonish
103. Times of day: Abbr.
104. Quandary
106. —— cloth
109. Hayworth
110. Charms, in London
112. Kind of gage
113. Writer Marsh and others
120. Old capital of Brittany
122. Footless
124. Copies
125. Ermine in summer
126. Bull: Prefix
127. Coincide
128. Succeed
130. Symbol of leakiness
132. Look like the ——
134. Ridge
135. Influenced
137. Betsy
139. Employs
141. —— bien
144. Auto dealer's abbreviation
145. Shipper's group: Abbr.
146. Titled Turk

Up and Away

by Cornelia Warriner

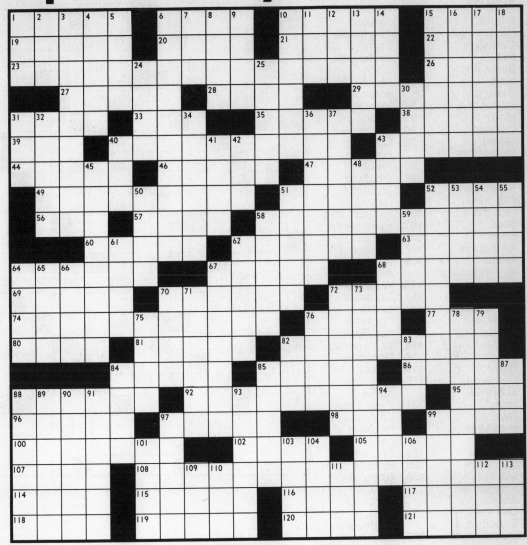

ACROSS

1. Le Mans entry
6. Tattle
10. Theda et al.
15. Down with: Fr.
19. Soap plant
20. Opera
21. Roman official
22. Bridge: Fr.
23. Subject of a Verne novel
26. Church booklet
27. Rule the —
28. Permeate
29. Navy specialists
31. Like falling off a log
33. Article
35. Take again
38. "—— Not Alone"
39. Poetic form
40. Name for early moon-bound spider's home
43. —— weensy
44. Billiard stroke
46. Lisa and others
47. Brazilian Indians
49. Preference
51. Month
52. Confound!
56. "—— had a million"
57. Party man
58. Ingredient of a satellite
60. Former V.I.P. at U.N.
62. Unpolished
63. Gladden
64. Taker
67. Footwear
68. Plays
69. Dog-tired
70. Leisured
72. Song
74. Mariner's job
76. Sped
77. Shoshonean
80. Soft-drink quality
81. Lariat
82. Separated
84. English dramatist
85. —— worms
86. Pine substance
88. First baseball czar
92. Certain V.I.P.'s
95. Blaster's need
96. New York city
97. "—— twig is..."
98. Shrewd
99. Grasslands
100. Glass, in pharmacy
102. Saarinen
105. Did dishes
107. Increase, old style
108. Assignment for the Apollo 11 men
114. One in ambush
115. Missouri tributary
116. Black: It.
117. Asian sorghum: Var.
118. Porsena
119. Salamanders
120. Coffee grind
121. Successful

DOWN

1. Rule, in India
2. I love: Lat.
3. "... —— the stars"
4. Man's name
5. Western city
6. "...be a dog and ——"
7. Eng. course
8. Flurries
9. Lessen
10. Phone sound device
11. Navy man: Abbr.
12. —— de Oro
13. In space
14. Classman: Abbr.
15. Point in orbit
16. One of trio on first moon orbit
17. Companion of 16 Down
18. Obdurate
24. Baltic state: Abbr.
25. Assembles
30. Has an obligation
31. July 31, for example: Abbr.
32. Cotton from Bengal
34. Selfish one
36. Labor pioneer
37. Architects' patterns
40. Private eye
41. Relatives, familiarly
42. West
43. Soft mineral
45. —— fire
48. Russian hemp
50. Flanged beam
51. Set —— of interest
52. "Au Clair ——"
53. Paper measure
54. Movie dog
55. Pipe joints
58. Brant
59. Man of the hour
61. Whetstone
62. Australian shrub
64. Bligh: Abbr.
65. —— breve
66. Flight ——
67. Medical assay
68. Three: Ger.
70. English painter
71. Musical syllables
72. Brown colors
73. Words for a good splashdown
75. Very: Fr.
76. State: Abbr.
78. Put through a dry run
79. Scottish city, to poets
82. —— Paulo
83. Alternatives
84. Evergreen
85. Inch along
87. Certain times: Abbr.
88. Gemini spaceman
89. Girl's name
90. Infernal
91. Brave ones
93. College chores
94. Beginner
97. Divert
99. Fruit
101. Preposition
103. Covering
104. River to the Baltic
106. Prefix for a country
109. Shooter
110. Deputy: Abbr.
111. Silkworm
112. Gold: Sp.
113. Fuzz

Wherewithal

by H.L. Risteen

ACROSS

1. Slight
5. Harbor sight
9. Carthage foe
13. Some doorbells
19. Olympian
21. Editor of a kind
23. Burger ballad
24. Plea of the '30s
27. Trades
28. Nobleman
29. Old-time reporter's goal
30. Edge
31. An Astaire
32. Prizes
35. Assemblage
36. Prefix for fit or factor
37. Old English letter
39. Makes turbid
40. Indian V.I.P.
41. Reduced
42. Common abbreviations
45. Mine passages
47. Hitler predecessor
48. Mark
50. An apostle: Abbr.
51. Old ——
52. Solicitudes
53. Dumas hero
57. "Exodus" hero
58. Portuguese money
59. French city
60. Aaron
62. Parseghian
63. Most rigid
65. French keys
66. Artery
67. Young animal
68. Bristles
69. Paired
70. Onward
71. —— majesty
72. Inconsistent
77. Monterrey money
78. Ventilator
79. —— of thought
80. Confuse
82. Insect
83. Fishing equipment
84. Of an arm bone
85. Salutation in Soissons
87. Dessert
88. Zoo attractions
89. Undergrad clubs
90. Moved, at sea
91. Merkel
92. Infer
94. Santa ——
95. Cobbler supplies
96. Fetch
97. Obscure
99. Troubles
100. Report
101. Exclamation
102. Farm areas
105. Flirts
107. Cross out
108. Folding money
110. Water birds
111. Crosscut saw
112. Doctor's needlework
114. Palm genus
118. Unburden
119. Frisky
120. Persian sprite
121. Pastry item
123. Words prior to being parted
128. Shore bird
129. Freckle
130. Grieg girl
131. Oriental rugs
132. U.S. engineer
133. Coal layer
134. Promontory

DOWN

1. Strand
2. Annoys
3. Disregard
4. Beverage
5. Ocean: Abbr.
6. Leave —— huff
7. Groups of nine
8. Old English coins
9. Stem: Prefix
10. Siamese coins
11. Rigging
12. Person of great wisdom
13. Athenian foe of Sparta
14. Bestow, as praise
15. Neither Dem. nor Rep.
16. Drudge
17. Small animal
18. Oozed
19. Eastern church title
20. Rooted custom: Abbr.
22. Rock pinnacles
25. Army man: Abbr.
26. Urban sunbath areas
33. Eastern notables
34. Obligation
35. Throws
36. Vamp of silents
38. Summons
40. Roman goddess
41. Alaskan attire
42. French political units
43. Middlesex
44. Mint worker
46. Dutch coin
47. Kennedy items
49. "We —— on like this"
51. Long —— (money)
52. Grow, as a vine
54. Earns, informally
55. Fabric
56. Marquis de
59. Fix a dress
60. Does a vaudeville turn
61. European river
64. Healthy: Sp.
65. Lawyers' staple
66. Tree
69. Gets stuck
70. Coins of India
71. Headwear: Slang
73. Noisy canine
74. Message
75. Western range
76. Byways
77. Cashier's stamp
81. Muse
83. Molten outpourings
84. Soviet range
85. Heavy knife
86. Public
89. Business gamble: Colloq.
90. Big hit
93. Roman period
94. Tropical plant
95. Pacific sea
98. Islamic text
100. Suite
101. Well-known Greek
102. Heavenly being
103. Toy
104. —— pools
106. Nondieter's friend
107. Farm animals
109. Holy Land man
111. Chicago team
112. Numerical prefix
113. Period
115. Kicks
116. Indonesian isle
117. Russian river
119. Russian whip
120. Sibilant signals
122. Asian land
124. Cells
125. State: Abbr.
126. High note
127. Vegetable

Digging into Things
by Ruth Ball

ACROSS

1. Glacial epoch
7. Quality
12. Setting for "Kate"
17. Well-excavated city of Egypt
18. —— mark
20. —— phrase
22. Paris subways
23. Experts in looking back
25. Belonging to: Suffix
26. Formerly, old style
27. Comes in last
28. Then, in France
29. Furnace man: Abbr.
30. Roistering
33. Theater area
34. Rain in Paris
35. "—— bug in . . .
37. Up
39. Amundsen and others
40. Shrewish ones
42. Shoe width: Abbr.
43. Eject
44. Mexican coins
45. Materials for a dig
51. French revolutionary family
53. Caravansary
54. Sullivan and others
55. —— machine
56. Gums: Prefix
57. Alpine tunnel
59. Endure: Scot.
60. Stratagem
61. Marionette maker
63. Man's name
64. Denials
65. Dwellings of a kind
66. Building beam
67. Potpourri
68. Really?
71. Grasp
72. Part of N.B.
73. Settled down
74. Stared
75. Overage
77. Moraine
80. Mountain in Greece
81. Le Gallienne and others
82. Boater
83. Clog in a way
85. Lorna and family
88. Watched the late show
90. "Beneath the —— frown he stands . . ."
93. Fragrant root
94. —— de deux
95. A geological age, for short
97. Famous Giant
99. 500 sheets
100. Confused skirmish
102. Golf positions
103. Earth
105. Locale for Schliemann
108. Ancient Cretan
109. Antelope of India
110. Dessert
111. Settle
112. Blinds, as a hawk
113. Rigid
114. Imminent

DOWN

1. Betels
2. Dark rocks
3. King in "Iliad"
4. ——cadabra
5. Certain scientists
6. Feminine suffix
7. Sculptured form
8. Clergyman
9. Residue
10. Sloping type: Abbr.
11. Locale of a Marx movie
12. Directions for readers: Abbr.
13. Before Sept.
14. Excavate in a special way
15. Destroy the spirit
16. Former Belgian queen
18. Clan identity
19. Rose-red dye
21. Blockheads
24. Tennis term
26. Mitigates
31. Aegean sight: Abbr.
32. Trash item
34. Elegant: Slang
36. Eye part
38. H.H. Munro
39. Charlotte ——
41. Word form for cave
43. Most peculiar
44. Proportionately
46. Ore deposit
47. Sea nymph
48. Germs
49. Gladdens
50. Slips
51. Pondering
52. —— of love
53. Elf
58. Marine fishes
59. Russ. river
62. Idol
64. Hitler
67. Spanish jars
68. Compute
69. Improved
70. Archaeologist's work
74. Fall guy
76. Rio's beach
78. Times of day
79. End slowly
80. Lily plants
84. —— be (in case)
85. Mark Van ——
86. Appetite, in psychology
87. Divine revelation
88. Of a Frankish people
89. Son of Poseidon
91. Impassable
92. Layers
94. Cosset
96. Saltpeter
98. Former Chief Justice
100. But, in Paris
101. Word in Mass. motto
104. Ref. work
106. Lace
107. Post: Abbr.
108. English teachers' group: Abbr.

Riddles

by Frances Hansen

ACROSS

1. Moved like a snail
6. Remove a cartridge primer
11. Wets down
16. "My Lord, —— Morning!"
21. Actress's helper
22. African antelope
23. —— of the finger
24. Took to court
25. Greek market
26. Enlarge
27. N.Z. native
28. Allow as how
29. Down-in-the-dumps lama?
31. Whirlybird hitchhiker?
34. Informal greetings
35. Thos. and others
36. Malaysian sir
37. Uneasy
38. —— date
40. Small plant leaf
42. Fatty
46. Unadorned convent headgear?
50. Constellation
53. Strong ——
54. Chemical suffix
55. Italian poet: 1754-1828
56. —— Mater
58. Persian fairy
59. Aim
61. Wee one
63. Becomes winter-bound
64. Footless animals
65. Cousin of a sari
66. Constant
67. Long distance, figuratively
68. Bit ——
69. Nimble
72. "Young Man of Caracas" author
74. José's aunt
76. Individual
77. Jaunty bird?
81. Tasteless
84. Corrida cry
85. Musical notes
86. Almond drink
88. City near Boys Town
89. Cup: Fr.
91. Hobo song words
93. First name in whodunits
95. Asian nurse
99. Organ parts
100. Bulk
101. Hugh Capet, for one
102. A Borgia
104. Type of billy
105. Makes fast a rope
106. Endured
108. Like Abner
109. New York Indian
111. Compass point
112. Excusable servant?
116. Certain beds
118. Dorm buddy
120. —— Mare
121. Makes tea
124. Chassé
125. —— Darya
126. Likely: Abbr.
130. Breakfast fish exporter
134. Brooding Indian
136. Jewish months
137. Lugger
138. Loup
141. Fragrant oil
142. Vocal style: Abbr.
143. Musical work
144. Confederate general
145. Fingerprint feature
146. Baltic people
147. She just growed
148. Hit a high fly ball
149. Roles

DOWN

1. Coarse fabric
2. Scoundrel
3. Hard wood
4. Brightens
5. Mine car
6. Petula Clark hit
7. Norse boys' names
8. El ——
9. Honest one
10. Hairnet's companion
11. Vic
12. Don't be ——!
13. Between I and r
14. Polynesian skirt
15. Flowering shrub
16. Unidentified one
17. Cheerful dad?
18. Take ——
19. Adjust
20. Mime
30. Bone: Greek
32. In the pink
33. Attacked
36. Kind of dance
39. Faucets and pipes: Abbr.
40. Zola
41. Spud grader
43. Small change in 25 Across
44. Piano mute: Sp.
45. Lived
46. Muslim title of respect
47. Don Juan's mother
48. Plateau
49. "Be —— so humble..."
51. See 2 Down
52. Red powder of India
56. Shoe, in Italy
57. Whensoever
60. Oil country: Var.
62. Chicken purchaser
63. —— man answers
64. Embarrass
66. Hard to pin down
70. Revolves
71. Native: Suffix
73. Mild rural expletives
75. Lupino
77. Saucepan ammunition?
78. Herb genus
79. Does a cobbler's job
80. Live teddy bears
82. Nymphette of fiction
83. Shoe widths
87. Scotch uncle
90. Cracked spar
92. Beauty spot
94. O'Grady
96. Bamako's country
97. "Questa o quella," for one
98. State of misery
102. Arise
103. Noble: Ger.
105. More plain
107. Ancient cast
110. Loathes
112. Yea or nay
113. Comes forth
114. Tuck's partner
115. Dry-cleaner
117. Sonnet part
119. Fish hawk
122. Snap
123. Watch the late show
125. Soap plant
127. Machine part
128. Modern paintings
129. Rolls a log
130. Poet Shapiro
131. French notion
132. Agreement
133. Jaywalkers: Abbr.
135. Bawl
139. Bird of prey, Cockney style
140. Ferdinand V

Capital Ideas

by Kirk Dodd

ACROSS

1. Hails
8. Cavies
13. Coin of Mid-East
20. Address loudly
21. People of Teheran
22. Plunge into a fluid
23. City in Granada
24. N.A. geological era
26. Grampus
27. Early Brazos settler
29. Moslem saint
30. Nobel physicist: 1952
32. Set a course
33. Heads
34. Middling
35. Hibernia
36. Styptic
37. Sheepfolds
38. Fountain orders
39. Children's game
41. City in West Germany
42. Satchel
43. Mean sea-level line
44. Interweave
45. Summon
46. Oddments
48. Beverages
49. One-time caller at Trinidad
53. Pea and nut
54. Erie, for one
55. Cracow people
56. Number
57. Strikes
58. Pebbles
60. Burma, Pakistan, etc.
61. Indian
62. Lemur
63. Aegean island
64. Perfume
65. Archipelago of Pacific
67. Grass genus
68. Ones at the helm
69. Elder: Fr.
70. Opted
71. American family of painters
72. Thin layer
75. Teen-agers' monopoly
76. Bewailed
79. Poplar
80. Opinions
81. Restrain
82. —— clock scholar
83. Soviet press agency
84. See eye ——
85. Productive
86. Hauls
87. High note
88. English essayist (1861-1922)
91. Agency of the 30s: Abbr.
92. Sec. of State under Wilson
94. Idle
96. Enliven: Lat.
97. Jog
98. Drain
99. Result of a salary cut
100. Rapiers
101. Encourages

DOWN

1. —— as a judge
2. Chaplin
3. Fruit
4. Inoperative
5. Cache
6. U.S. sculptor
7. Like some churches
8. Biblical treasure city
9. Court decree: Fr.
10. French city
11. Nova Scotia's —— Royal
12. Located
13. Liquid measures: Fr.
14. Kaffir fighters
15. Word of concurrence
16. Indian weight
17. Locale in Marine song
18. Peacocks
19. Emblem of 15th century
25. "Drang nach ——"
28. Rel. of sing.
31. Barley and rye
34. Oregon city
36. Vis- ——
37. Dances
38. Sorcerer
40. "——, sorry"
41. Of a space
42. Dells
44. Inclinations
45. Presidential family
46. Second-stringer
47. Tropical raccoon
48. Dyeing technique
49. Beverage
50. Dog
51. Eastern Christian
52. Torrefies
54. Siren of "Odyssey"
55. Ceremony: Fr.
58. Novel heroine
59. Poker move
60. Mollusk genus
62. Singer Frankie
64. Leeds's river
66. Postal system
67. Does an after-sports routine
68. Quince, for example
70. Indian
71. Girl's name
72. Pitchout, in football
73. Ear shell
74. Ore range
75. Famous sculpture
76. Guipure
77. Understanding
78. Prescription units
80. Kind of ball
81. Low parts of ships
84. Czech range
85. Meander
86. Western attire
88. Garment
89. Lie at anchor
90. Leaves
93. Type measures
95. Winter topic of talk

Colorful Airs

by Anne Fox

ACROSS

1. Sailors' drink
5. Monkey
10. Half of a magic formula
15. Wheedle
21. San ——
22. Oriental rug
23. Man of Meshed
24. Cut out
25. Hindu god
26. Music by Cole Porter
29. Moves furtively
31. Apiece
32. Levee
33. Up ——
34. Pacific org.
35. Bone
38. Meet
39. Piano piece
41. Card game
43. Sew up
45. Mogul
49. Music by Gershwin
54. Dance
55. Irish exclamation: Var.
56. "Conning Tower" man
57. British marshal of W.W.I.
58. Gelid
59. Barrier of physics
60. Keepsake
62. Apocrypha books: Abbr.
63. Half of a musical
64. Capers
65. Somewhat
66. Capuchins
68. Theater ticket bargains
70. Cliff dwelling
71. Clash
72. S.A. weapon
74. Runabout
75. Fur
76. Song of 1862
80. Defense group
84. Baleful
86. Old pottery pail
87. Clumsy fellow
88. U.S.A. rank
89. Nonsense!
92. Recanted, in a way
95. Gypsy: Fr.
96. Art form
97. Exclamation of disgust
99. Fall guy
100. Musical of 1933
101. Téte-à-téte
102. Musical syllable
103. White House tenant
104. Gas: Prefix
105. Family members: Abbr.
106. Dub
107. Lyrics by Mitchell Parish
111. Zinc
113. Sea birds
114. Punk
115. A Chaplin
116. Zip
117. Lowlander
119. Mediterranean ship
123. War
126. Cartoonist Addams
128. Gumbo
129. State of India
130. Part of "Annie Laurie"
136. An age
137. —— middle course
138. Golden
139. Manifest
140. Dare, old style
141. Residue
142. American poetess
143. Spanish port
144. Letters

DOWN

1. Shade of green
2. Rule: Fr.
3. Vincit —— veritas
4. Part of an academy song
5. Bulges
6. Kirghiz city
7. Guevara
8. Round Table knight
9. Giraffe's cousin
10. Wharf
11. Sphere
12. —— Forks (B.C. battle)
13. Dark
14. Material
15. Navy initials
16. Wild sheep
17. Music by Hoagy Carmichael
18. —— about
19. Unaspirated
20. Arctic island
27. Return partner's suit
28. Tenfold
30. Eyelid darkener
35. Allegro, for one
36. Pelvic bones
37. Containers: Abbr.
38. Dance
40. Kind of ball
42. Strapping
44. Town wear of song
45. Edging
46. Mood
47. Agalloch
48. Turns left
49. Witches
50. One of the Du Ponts
51. Italian condiment
52. Thai language
53. Offer
59. Talent
61. Scotch refusal
62. Poetic times
63. Holm
64. Fairbanks
66. Fortify
67. Pronoun
69. W.W. II initials
71. Guys
73. Under way
76. Ency. ——
77. Uh-huh
78. Swat
79. Principle
81. Incense holder of old Rome
82. Drum
83. An enzyme
85. Wild goat
88. Game shot
89. Position tracker
90. Group of Islamic savants
91. Iroquoian
93. Old Rhodes sight
94. Japanese ware
95. Not with it
96. Slam
98. Chin
100. Actress Ada
102. Wallop
103. Salon item, for short
104. Vapor: Prefix
107. Languid
108. Ease
109. Duty
110. Cunning
112. Old fogy
116. Prize
118. For this: Lat.
120. Cheap merchandise
121. Worn at the edges
122. Coins
123. Go by
124. Flower: Prefix
125. Item sometimes big
127. Piece of metal
128. Mickey and family
129. Capital of Moselle
131. Cape
132. German dessert
133. Girl's name
134. Florid
135. Son of Gad

Sizing Things Up

by Eva Pollack Taub

ACROSS

1. Skirt
7. Indian weight
11. Greatest
15. Man with a sword
16. Arithmetic device
19. Nonentity
21. Well-known Cockney
23. Bird
24. Canals on U.S. border
25. Mean abode
26. Track
27. Evergreen
28. Helper: Abbr.
30. Forbearance
32. Place for a barbecue
34. Home buyer's concern: Abbr.
35. Luster
37. Give the go-by
39. Meaning
41. Buddhist temple
42. Plumber's concern
45. "—— corny as . . ."
47. Role in "Barber of Seville"
49. On the loose
52. Planet
54. Word in a Hardy title
56. Greek letter
57. ". . . we all do fade as ——"
59. Disturb
61. Embankments
63. Recent: Prefix
64. Kingfish
65. Fastened
67. One of the Three Stooges
68. Groups: Abbr.
70. Town on the Hudson
73. Secular
74. Girl's name
76. Swelling disease of fish
77. Early age
79. English river
80. Postulate
82. Slack part of a sail
83. Minor

prophet
84. Noun suffix
85. Writ against a debtor
87. Nickname for Miss Ederle
89. Fabrics
91. One who makes up
93. State: Abbr.
94. Hostess's request
95. Container
97. Flint: Prefix
99. Swedish chemist
101. Gladden
105. Word element for a country
107. Silent star
109. Plants of a region
112. Caledonian
113. Charge
115. Scratchers
117. Dunne
119. Chem. prefix
120. Bridge moves
121. Broadway play of 1953
124. Flowers
125. Design
126. Bull-like
127. Tree toad
128. Modern concern
129. People of a world area

DOWN

1. Winter footwear
2. Indolent
3. Bolivia's La ——
4. Esau's wife
5. Biblical locale
6. Treasure ——
7. Ballerina Maria
8. Sash
9. Plaster backing
10. Misbehave
11. Star in Cetus
12. A kind of den
13. Gear for hams
14. Russian cart
15. Flat-topped hills
17. Bones
18. Dog
19. Vast
20. Lease again
22. Poetic words
29. Tissue: Anat.
31. Arizona city
33. Privy to
36. Chemical liquid
38. Village in New York
40. Vain: Ger.
43. Shining
44. Wailed
46. Thick-set
48. Of snow
49. City in

Illinois
50. French saint
51. Area of Queens, N.Y.
53. Scout activity
55. Strangest
58. Dye workers
60. Slow, in music
62. Chinese mediums of exchange
65. Abdomen: Prefix
66. River of Ukraine
69. Weather word
71. Ex-film star Jack
72. Taunts
75. Ancient Greek city
78. Unworldly
81. Tim's quality
83. Feature
86. End: Pref.

88. Unhearing
90. Army men: Abbr.
92. Boxing jabs
95. Headpiece
96. Not on credit
98. Sound like an old door
100. Japanese seaweed
102. Colorless liquid
103. Subway items
104. Storehouse
106. European thrush
108. Signed in a way
110. Lariat
111. Indian coins
114. Fluids
116. Bristle: Prefix
118. Small case
122. Richthofen, for one
123. Relative of Mme.

Working People
by Thomas W. Schier

ACROSS

1. Smooth off
7. Lugosi
11. Marlowe, for one
15. Living quarters: Abbr.
19. Minnesota Fats, for one
20. Michigan's waterfront
21. Pack animal
22. Kind of hog
23. Offer a legal excuse
24. Heath genus
25. Faust
27. Memorable play of 1946
30. Brand of figs
31. Attach firmly
32. Staff officers
33. Sets ——
37. Neck wrap
38. Glacial ridges
40. Luminous circles
43. Mediocre
44. Campus building
45. Kind of jacket
48. Door-to-door lads
51. Overly bland
55. Hip bones
56. Word of mouth
57. Bristle
58. Elevation: Abbr.
59. Doing: Suffix
61. Collaborator
63. Slope, in fortification
67. Merry-andrew
69. Exclamation
70. Teachers' org.
71. African javelin
72. From —— Z
73. Makes a scene
75. Foggy
77. Danish coin
78. Bell sound
81. Well-known Russian
85. Ripened
86. Prefix with corn or form
87. Illinois first name
88. Hercules's captive and others
89. Jack in

cribbage
91. "—— du Printemps"
93. Navy man: Abbr.
96. Peas or beans: Abbr.
97. Musical composition
101. African fetish
102. Glad, to poets
103. Swedish town
104. Stake
105. Pronoun
106. Item in a bibliothèque
108. Cordelia's father
110. Onlooker
113. Cooper man
117. Find by chance
118. Raceway event
119. City in West
120. Candy
122. Lawyers: Abbr.
126. Wheel part
127. Petitions
129. Town of Asia Minor (Latin sp.)
131. This, in old Rome
132. Metal piece
134. John Gay opus
139. Hothouse workers
143. Negative contraction
144. Type of decoration
145. In —— shell
146. Bell town
147. Yes
148. ——-camp
149. Fabric
150. Sounds for attention
151. Kind of tube
152. Coin user of a sort

DOWN

1. Cards in a low straight
2. Garden features
3. Grayish-green
4. Mine: Fr.
5. Eastern ketch
6. Nine: Prefix
7. Stove part
8. Discoverer of Vinland
9. Part of a train, for short
10. P.I. sumac
11. —— pencil
12. Fragment
13. Offend
14. Extremely
15. Military acronym
16. Hairdo
17. Quivering motions
18. Rivulet
20. Leave port
21. English spa
26. Calm area
28. Unit of metric length
29. Word for annual winds
34. Flanders Field symbol
35. Sailing
36. Newsman
39. Helpers of Drs.
41. Excluding both
42. Piercing

tool
44. Sweet: It.
46. Pismire
47. Chauffeurs of a sort
49. Fence part
50. Domineering
51. —— Mahal
52. Be obligated
53. Cricket sides
54. Spring wild flower
60. Impossible
62. Gambler's mecca
64. Excited
65. Like Ben Jonson
66. Variegated
68. Child's game
71. Month: Abbr.
73. Electronics initials
74. Member of a Burmese people
76. Western group:

Abbr.
78. Sofian: Abbr.
79. Unique person
80. Unless: Lat.
82. Cheer
83. Copter, at times
84. "—— Three Lives"
85. Man's nickname
87. Pungent
90. Surpass
92. Metal point
94. Sourpuss
95. 4,840 square yards
98. Jutting rock
99. Clumsy boat
100. Noun suffix
102. Household plants
104. Item for a leaky boat
107. Steam
109. Consort of Shamash
111. Sheathed
112. Spanish

queen
113. Champion of the people
114. Batter's quest
115. Palliates
116. Forest group
118. Threefold
121. French historian
123. "...—— a way"
124. Harangue
125. Alpine figure
127. Soul: Fr.
128. Surprised exclamation
130. —— as a pig
133. Concerning
135. Rope fiber
136. Wyandot's cousin
137. Miscellany
138. Siliques
140. Beat the
141. Prison areas: Abbr.
142. Interweave

Taking a Position
by Threba Johnson

ACROSS

1. Hero of Greek legend
5. Shakespearean shepherdess
10. Himalayan animal
17. Alaskan city
18. Order: Fr.
20. Madison Ave. thinkers
21. Author O'Connor
22. Goodman book
25. Making a thrust
27. Cassia plants
28. Wrong: Prefix
29. —— cantorum
30. Like: Suffix
31. Welsh name
33. Racetrack pests
37. Negrito
38. Theologian of 16th cent.
41. Alike: Fr.
43. Old weapon
44. Choices: Abbr.
46. Conditions
47. Gounod's "—— et Baucis"
50. Army medal
51. Means of transportation
54. French season
55. Skilled interpreter
57. Marquis de ——
58. Initials on an airline board
59. Backed a cause
61. S.A. catfish
62. Kind of eclipse
64. 1949 treaty
66. Word of respect in India
68. Feminine suffix
69. Epitaph for a movie palace
74. Preposition
75. Divinity degree
76. Majority
77. Do a grammar chore
78. Mexican Indian
80. Hinder legally
82. Sit-down result
84. Vestments
86. On the —— a wave
88. Letter
89. Slight
91. U.S. dept.
92. Devices for catching fish
95. Pique
96. Homeless tot
98. Rat- ——
100. Nautical term
101. "No" voter
104. Road: Abbr.
105. —— the land
107. Testing places
109. Long time
110. Sell: Fr.
112. Young seal
114. Rattle on a harness
116. Subscription affair
117. On Cloud 9
122. Part of to have: Fr.
123. Without means of rowing
124. One-up word
125. Bow man
126. Circuses
127. Momentum
128. Places of refuge

DOWN

1. Ones called for service
2. Leonard Woolf book
3. Mexican friend
4. Of old age
5. Steal, in Scotland
6. 1949 peace Nobelist
7. Toast
8. Cinched
9. Have —— ear
10. Sleeper
11. Dutch cheese
12. Ledger entry
13. Singers
14. Large bird
15. Gas: Prefix
16. 3 mins. of boxing: Abbr.
19. Nine: Prefix
21. Maxwell and others
23. Called to order
24. Treatment
26. Village of East Bengal
30. Caucasus native
32. Some social climbers
34. Rostin book
35. With a will
36. One who quits
39. Miller play
40. Part of a Goldsmith title
42. Smoked salmon
45. Diligent
48. Adjective suffix
49. Composer Rorem
52. Medical prefix
53. Borge
56. Obeys a street sign
60. Compass reading
63. Sternward
65. A king of Egypt
67. "—— body meet . . ."
69. Madeira port
70. Inimical planet
71. Pinafore
72. French town
73. Soviet range
79. Lawyer: Abbr.
81. Darkness
83. Par ——
85. Sports areas
87. Danish money
90. Pass a rope through
93. Fruit
94. Make oneself heard
97. Senses
99. Formal wear
102. Regulate
103. Tebaldi
106. Code, in Spanish law
108. Are: Fr.
111. To no extent
113. Kind of school
115. N.M. colony
116. Marsh grass
117. Central area
118. Zoology suffix
119. Biblical prince
120. Football scores: Abbr.
121. Article

No Extra Charge
by W.E. Jones

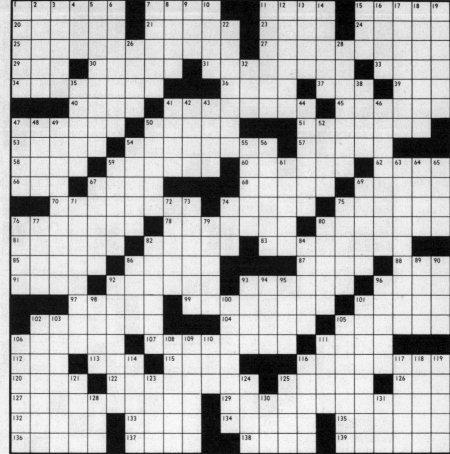

ACROSS

1. Character in "Faerie Queene"
7. Lombardy lake
11. Iceland epic
15. Concentrates
20. Layer
21. States
23. Money's offshoot
24. Yoga posture
25. Acrobatic bookkeeping
27. Wall St. prefix
29. Calendar abbr.
30. Sell —— of goods
31. The's, e.g.
33. During
34. Head areas
36. The —— of Tempe
37. Spire ornament
39. Direction
40. Pulitzer author, 1958
41. Advisory groups
45. Finished the laundry
47. Relatives
50. Of melody
51. Graduation guests
53. Hogarth men
54. Buck
57. That is: Lat.
58. Defeats at bridge
59. Moon goddess
60. 40,000—— (big ship)
62. Genus of bees
66. —— bonne heure
67. Mailed
68. Makes a stab at
69. Belief
70. Slow as
74. Grants
75. Shed copiously
76. Inspire
78. Of heat
80. Costa Rica export
81. Takes a new tenant
82. Tunneled
83. Formality
85. Cooking byproducts
86. Panama

port
87. Roman jug
88. Dock: Abbr.
91. —— everything
92. Flair
93. ". . .—— trash"
96. Relative of zool.
97. Special drink
99. Symbol of wealth
101. Cavity: Anat.
102. Stars, for Cicero
104. Port where Greeks sailed for Troy
105. Most feeble
106. Of the wrist
107. Poured
111. Town in Hungary
112. Wine vessel
113. His: Fr.
115. Chinese dynasty
116. Student's emblem
120. Wash: Lat.
122. Mozart opus
125. Contradict
126. City in

Korea
127. Modern Aladdin's lamp
129. Has it made
132. Publicized
133. Batting backstop
134. Water wheel
135. Long time for poets
136. Eastern civet
137. Stettin's river
138. Tiresias was one
139. Large basket

DOWN

1. Illinois city
2. Polo
3. Leaves undone
4. Inlet
5. Blows up
6. Cats
7. Puts and
8. Athletic field
9. "Testimony of Two ——"
10. Killer whale
11. Chancel

seat
12. Shore bird
13. A type of net
14. Lane: Fr.
15. Golf goal
16. Mountain in Thessaly
17. Garb
18. Jets, e.g.
19. Worked on floors
22. Sycophantic
26. Wing: Fr.
28. Ambitious one
32. Color
35. Extra jurors
38. Angers
41. —— about
42. Presently
43. Bundle
44. Quills
46. Toronto man
47. —— Major
48. A season
49. Provide a treat of sorts
50. Jousts
52. Drinks
54. That makes
55. Mink's relative
56. Eric, for one

59. Landed estates
61. Relative
63. Smart to a point
64. Concept
65. Fixes a lawn
67. Flaps violently
69. Boat
71. Go too far
72. Elève's school
73. Wraparound
74. Cape
75. Grand Central feature
76. Cupid
77. Mother of Castor
79. Slowly: Music
80. Pretty one, in Rome
82. Fled
84. Passages
86. —— Grande
89. Cowpoke's mount
90. Level
92. Most improbable
93. Rabbit's tail
94. Lacquered ware
95. Writer Bagnold

96. Machetes
98. Waves: Sp.
100. Comedian of silent films
101. Tiny Tim's voice
102. Biblical city of Palestine
103. Name in golf Hall of Fame
105. Extolled
106. Spur: Biol.
108. Develop
109. Live coal
110. Noun suffix
111. Friend
114. Dry: It.
116. Romero
117. Landing places
118. Goddess of peace
119. Saltpeter
121. Horace's metier
123. South African assembly
124. Son of Seth
125. Biscay, to the French
128. Chemical suffix
130. Before
131. —— publica

Looking Sharp

by A.J. Santora

ACROSS

1. Señor's talk
6. Throwback
13. The —— luxury
18. Bargains
19. Suite
20. Type of ether
21. Broadway name
23. Collier
24. In trouble
25. Bit of reading
27. Compass point
28. Great miler
29. Impudence
31. Slithery
32. Mineo and namesakes
33. Credibility ——
34. Stitch for samplers
38. Plains Indian
40. Senior member
41. Part of R.B.I.
42. Bedrock
43. Quenched
45. Kind of rug
47. Heraldic fur
48. Fearful
49. Recoil
50. Neapolitan, for one
54. Pitch pipe
55. Glances of a kind
57. Holiday time
58. Floodlights
59. Mexican mullet
60. Fit to ——
61. Entrance
62. "—— Got Rhythm"
63. Led the attack
67. Threadlike
68. Tints over
70. Paid up
71. Winner of olés
72. Siouan
73. Grand and others
75. Dissenting view
76. Book section
78. Carry: Lat.
79. Bridge seats
80. Hang fire
82. 1926 Pulitzer novel
84. Cheer
87. Cupid
88. Philippine tree
90. Suffix for gang or trick
91. Irritate: Colloq.
92. Word connector
93. Library worker
96. "—— tennis?"
99. Foolish
101. Overhead liability
103. Ground quartz
104. Reprimand
105. Commiserates
106. Delicious
107. Certifies
108. Word on a French map

DOWN

1. Out at the elbows
2. The Veep
3. Ironside of TV
4. Table extender
5. Pitched in
6. Custody
7. Ball holder
8. "Take —— from me"
9. Passport entry
10. Approximately
11. Boulevard of note
12. Decoration
13. Court marker
14. Mon ——
15. Support for edgy people
16. Pull —— (tease)
17. Anticipate
18. Chekhov
—. Uncle
21. Small town
22. Instruct
26. —— joint
30. Released: Colloq.
32. Affirm
34. Stud or draw
35. Seen
36. Weight
37. Circle or sanctum
39. Guinness et al.
40. Defies
43. Road turn
44. Army men
45. Severity
46. Disturbed the peace
47. Dog, for short
48. Step
49. River of a blues song
51. Campus girl
52. Zoo adjunct
53. Paris version of IRT
55. Active one
56. Takes aboard
59. Elks
61. Buenos ——
63. U.S. painter and illustrator
64. Inimical one
65. Don's January
66. Stocks selling —— (bear market)
67. Onward
69. Mink's cousin
71. Tryout
74. Pertaining to uprising
75. Figure in O'Neill play
76. Rubinstein
77. Cleaning aid
79. Correct
81. Dit's companion
82. Way off beam
83. Groups of aides
84. M-16's
85. Pale green
86. Possessive
89. Jai-alai gear
91. Brief novel
93. Relative of sultry
94. Gardner
95. Relatives of TV's: Abbr.
97. Skip
98. —— chance
100. Profit
102. Poetic word

Rhymes from Way Out by Edward J. O'Brien

ACROSS

1. Amphibians
6. Relative: Abbr.
9. Of a Mideast nation
15. "It's —— story"
19. —— gatherum
21. Did a farm job
22. Mexican lady
23. Went on horseback
24. Refusal to a Friday hold-up man
27. Relative of a cockney 'ero
28. Exclamation of surprise
29. Grain
30. Relatives of orgs.
31. Structures of like origin
33. Rio's —— Açúcar
35. Entertain lavishly
39. Centers
41. Dionnes' doctor
42. Part of an English county
43. Words for a cabled smoke signal
46. Possess: Scot.
47. Living-room eyes
51. Church court
52. "...in deepest grief ——"
55. Electrical unit
56. Party
57. Sand ridge
58. Certain words: Abbr.
60. Prevail
61. Duo
63. Word after waste and want
64. French friend
66. Chair
67. Berle, for short
68. Novel
70. Scot's denial
72. Life ins. man
74. Energy: Abbr.
75. Throat, in England
76. Clerical union's demand for a raise
82. One who keeps 64th notes
83. Words for a navigator's role
84. Now
85. Against
86. Three, in Rome
87. Fast plane: Abbr.
88. She: Ger.
89. Speeds
90. Wan
91. "A rose —— rose"
93. Fireproof material: Abbr.
95. Plant beards
98. Balaam's transport
99. Whitney
100. Droop
102. Consecrate
105. Misfortune
106. Earthquake: Prefix
109. Extracted
111. Ridicule (with "of")
112. Charlemagne domain: Abbr.
113. No. 1 airport runway
116. Do —— turn
118. Paints
120. Poetic adverbs
121. Took out
124. New Deal name
125. One more
127. Points
129. Shoe size
131. "When I was ——"
132. Aqua ——
133. Forecast for a poor shoe repair
139. Flying initials
140. Excite
141. Roman date
142. Tuneful
143. Soccer star
144. Couch
145. Receive
146. Suffered

DOWN

1. Leading mod art store
2. Laughter in Nebraska
3. Dictum of a prudish girl watcher
4. Nursery words
5. Latin possessive
6. Lad
7. Kind of pronoun: Abbr.
8. Harem room
9. "There —— answer"
10. Try to attain
11. Hearts, clubs, or whatever
12. Digits: Abbr.
13. Poker player's words
14. Coral islets
15. Have —— for (esteem)
16. Comment on how part of an audience will react
17. Bell town
18. Slow-witted
20. Muscle: Prefix
21. Despise
25. Conflict
26. French river
32. Norse god
34. Corporation levies: Abbr.
36. Earth goddess
37. Girl's name
38. Fleur-de-
40. Heroic sea rescue
44. Time period
45. Old form of be
48. Long time
49. Thrifty
50. Words for a star at liberty
53. Castor bean
54. In the earth: Fr.
57. Large steam shovel
59. "—— Wimpole Street"
62. Eye parts
65. Woodchuck
66. Chair backs: Var.
67. Fever disease
69. Like a V-shaped object
71. Flemish name of Ixelles
73. Brimless hats
75. Waters
76. Start of some riddles
77. Abelard's beloved
78. These: Fr.
79. Of age: Abbr.
80. French pronoun
81. Royal initials
90. Laborer
92. City in Turkey
94. Heat measure: Abbr.
96. Out of fish eggs, too
97. Shabby feat
100. Rational
101. Reverence
103. —— out
104. Hindu grant
107. N.M. capital
108. Before mash
110. Jogged some
111. Damage
114. Region of France
115. —— majesty
117. Travel briefly
118. Slurp
119. Occupied
122. Lampreys
123. State: Abbr.
126. Food: Slang
128. Fr. miss
130. Oahu town
134. Scrap
135. Lively dance
136. Poem
137. Wager
138. Conjunctions

Around the House by Emanuel Berg

ACROSS

1. Projects
5. Went hot-rodding
10. Investment item
15. Merganser
19. Biblical giant
20. Allen
21. Lombardi
22. Greek liqueur
23. —— et orbi
24. "—— human hopes"
26. Sinn ——
27. Not any, in law
28. "—— were the days"
29. Holm oak
30. S.A. plains
32. It's yet to come
34. Tennis points
35. Matches up
36. Starchy plant
37. Beaverlike
39. Tasteful
42. Do-nothing
45. Arctic sight
46. Wine: Prefix
47. Sheol and others
48. Silver: Abbr.
49. Droplet
50. Soil science: Abbr.
51. Havens
52. Pairs
53. Nearer
55. Bishopric
56. Shofar
57. Nandus
58. Pacific isles
62. Fit to drink
64. Pass off (with "on")
65. Disappeared
66. Guarantee
67. Gay
68. European capital
69. Writer Victor, to cockneys
70. Reaction
72. Roric
73. Cinch
74. Surveyed the joint
77. Track
78. —— with (favor)
79. Wood: Prefix
80. Gluck
81. Drum staves
82. Unpopular bird
84. Lung ailment

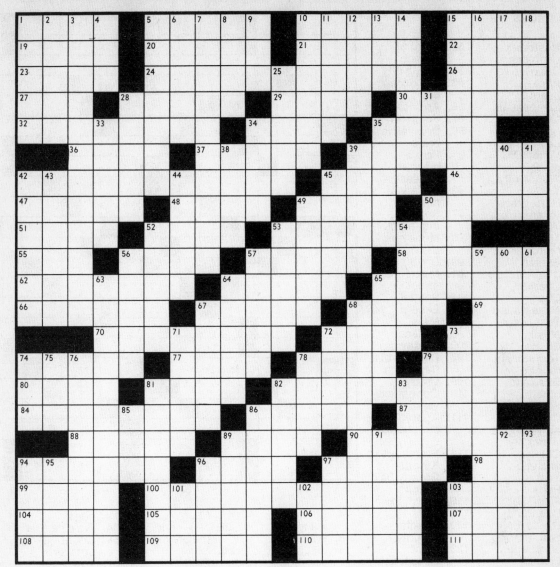

86. Boa
87. Vex
88. Poignant
89. Clever move
90. Resembling the Acropolis
94. Artist's pad
96. Auction word
97. Field mice
98. Dirigible, for short
99. Bowfin genus
100. Pasquinaders
103. Hand: Sp.
104. Type of etching
105. Irregular
106. Siren signal
107. African antelope
108. Nervous
109. Stormed
110. Western sights
111. June 6, 1944

DOWN

1. Brief trip
2. California's Jesse ——
3. Deipnosophists
4. Sports gear
5. Hurl again
6. Musketeer
7. Father Brown's creator
8. Roof part
9. Life-essential acid
10. More sinister
11. Takes the hook
12. Chalcedony
13. Army grade: Abbr.
14. Collapse
15. Fine till now
16. Kind of cheese

17. Pinza
18. Tony of early radio
25. More subtle
28. Pressure units
31. First-century date
33. Keens
34. Field: Lat.
35. Search into
38. Iowa city
39. At —— for words
40. Daughter of Cadmus
41. Against
42. Dance step
43. From —— in
44. —— thing
45. Fishing bob
49. Hallowed
50. When the scholar used to come
52. Handouts

53. Animal's spine
54. Pluvial
56. Engaged
57. Dinner course
59. Parlor Romeo
60. Lake near Como
61. Visit
63. Rule of too many thumbs
64. Suomi people
65. Wooden pin
67. Covered with a cosmetic
68. Garden plot
71. Aspect
72. Fashion name
73. Seal
74. Mushroom part
75. Word with

out or aboard
76. Vilifying
78. Cask part: Scot.
79. Columbia team
81. Golfer Gene
82. Italian coin
83. Churchmen
85. Herb
86. Flew, in a way
89. Small wood
91. Extreme
92. African country
93. Kind of resin
94. Stare
95. Surrounded by
96. City problem
97. Mean
101. Sky Altar
102. Business org.
103. Up-to-date

Executive Suite

by Ross L. Jamison Jr.

ACROSS

1. Nestors
6. Latin dance
11. Cut over
16. Prickly pears
21. Lambeau of football fame
22. Lag behind
23. Venetian medal
24. French city
25. Yucca
27. Hard-times token
29. Yutang
30. Throat feature
31. French drink
32. Charlie Chan exclamation
33. Tennessee player
34. Elixirs
36. Tournament rounds
38. Baba and others
39. Simple
40. Unemployed
41. Water lily
42. Coldly analytic
44. Year, in Paris
46. Five-spot
47. Changing the decor
49. San Antonio attraction
52. Lament
53. Monitor lizard
55. Prospector's find
56. Grant an extension
57. Enterprise
59. Danube tributary
60. Townsman
62. Root
63. Limestone formation
65. Complete costume
66. Windy City, for short
67. Household member
68. Scandinavian
70. Duo
71. U.S. time zone: Abbr.
74. Spider monkey
76. Precious stone
78. Bring upon
80. Word of assent
81. Italian city
83. Old Roman day
85. Answer
87. Pat gently
89. Decorative braid
91. Parliament of Mideast
93. Variety of cherry
97. Spanish mining city
98. Money on the Corso
99. Drive
101. Memphis street
102. Spatial
104. Ekberg
105. Metal fastener
106. Oakley
107. Relative of a flapjack
109. Crafty
110. Opposite of verso
111. Approached, poetically
113. Storehouse
115. Kingfish
116. Galway Bay islands
118. Czech town
119. Old
120. Fought roughly
123. Bribe
124. Possessive
125. Footlike part
126. Confederate general
128. Sea union: Abbr.
129. Woman's coverall
132. Chinese vermilion
134. Chemical compound
135. Cavity
136. Immense expanse
137. Singer Della
138. Courser
139. Kind of drum
140. One of the strings
141. Skaldic poetry

DOWN

1. Brave's trophy
2. TV section
3. Subsidy
4. Shade maker
5. Cardiologist's concern
6. British guns
7. Bellicose god
8. Huckster's milieu
9. Lodging place
10. Tankard contents
11. Cookie of baseball
12. Son of Isaac
13. Moment, for short
14. Former Detroit slugger
15. Site of Statuary Hall
16. Third word of "Aeneid"
17. Kind of lamp
18. Carriage horse
19. Quartet member
20. Cordage fiber
26. "—— but the brave"
28. Bone: Prefix
31. Outer garments
35. Similar in action
37. Graz's river
38. Set straight
39. He-devil
41. River to Gulf of Gaeta
42. Thatch grasses
43. —— diem
44. Moslem V.I.P.
45. One of the Parcae
46. Kismet
48. Spanish peso
50. Ear of corn, in Africa
51. Proprietors
53. Bravery
54. New word: Abbr.
58. Fish afflictions
61. Parthenogenetic
64. Zig's partner
65. Counting-out word
67. Town near Sacramento
69. Atlantic sea bird
71. Winter melon
72. Filched
73. "Grass Harp" author
75. Forage plant
77. Singer Torme
79. —— avis
82. Fermi's nationality
84. Sully
86. Variety of cotton
88. Superiors
90. Revoke a legacy
92. Operatic piece
93. Infested with tiny insects
94. English breed of cattle
95. Yokel
96. Aware of
98. Release
100. Mah-jongg piece
103. Sudden collapse
108. Greek letter
110. Put back
112. Eggs: Ger.
114. Region of France
115. Mutts
116. Residue
117. Resting place
119. Awareness
120. Early Haitian Indian
121. Ancient city of Syria
122. Certain ranchers
124. Flock
125. Rain hard
127. Soviet range
130. Victory sign
131. Cell constituent
132. Ad ——
133. Man's nickname

Showing the Way
by Nancy Schuster

ACROSS

1. Add more stickum
8. Recital pieces
14. Ivan's villa
19. In
20. More annoyed
22. Chills
23. Prisoners of a kind
25. —— Bulba
26. Prayer form
27. Tie up
28. Brontë heroine
30. Number prefix
31. Collection of sayings
32. Beaux ——
34. —— sack
36. Substitute
38. Canasta play
40. Fine fur
41. Entree
43. Manner
44. Sandy ridge
46. Latticework
48. Of a grain
50. Wire measures
52. Paris name
53. Losing money
56. Sink fixtures
59. Nervous walking
61. Signore's land
62. Try to outdo
63. Pale
65. Part of the forest scene
66. Branch of peace
67. "—— corny as..."
69. Wire: Abbr.
71. African antelope
73. River to North Sea
74. Baseball hit
76. Long-beaked Atlantic fish
78. Passion
80. Sounds of hesitation
81. Color
82. Bears, mice and pigs
84. Elicitors
86. Skyline sights
88. Drooping
90. Pseudo-esthetic
91. Composer
92. Popular dosage
94. Radical in famed 1921 trial
98. Wings
100. Pants
102. Whale
104. Splash over
105. Briefcase item
107. Weaken
108. Some poultry
110. Cockney's distress cry
111. Tending to: Suffix
112. Lancaster
114. Waters: Sp.
116. Ethiopian town
118. "—— the West Wind"
120. Covert
123. TV fare
124. Early epoch
125. Retinue
126. Wood nymph
127. Caught
128. Frightened, hillbilly style

DOWN

1. Publicity
2. Lancelot's love et al.
3. Part of a coach's job
4. Official deeds
5. Goad
6. Zero and successors in "Fiddler"
7. Dutch commune
8. Crowned a certain way
9. 1900-mile Asian river
10. Protection
11. Polka dot on a garment, in a way
12. Article in Bonn
13. Move back
14. Office stamp
15. Moslem title
16. Animal act, usually
17. Beating items
18. Official edict
21. Alfonso, for one
24. Perfume
29. Met again
33. Prepares
35. Scientific group: Abbr.
37. Agreeably
39. John's predecessor
41. "Half ——"
42. Involved explanation
45. Baltic gulf
47. Back talk
49. Chemical prefix
51. At sea
53. —— form
54. Young eels
55. Textile workers
56. Apish
57. "Louder-and funnier" area
58. Biblical pauses
60. Kansas college
62. Early movie name
64. Prefix for a body net-work
68. Cut off
70. Stage cover
72. Gloomy
75. Italian painter
77. Barks
79. Enlistees: Abbr.
83. —— -disant
85. Nestling
87. Former Indian leader
89. Charged a certain way
92. Gardner
93. Kind of potato
95. Detergent
96. University unit
97. Resisting
98. Furnish
99. More clashing
101. Nautical direction
103. "—— Krupp"
106. Popular investment
108. Soft candy
109. —— Coeur
113. Baseball data: Abbr.
115. Pesty bug
117. "—— horse!"
119. Philippine tree: Var.
121. Garden tool
122. Old Gov't. agency

OutYonder

by Mary M. Murdoch

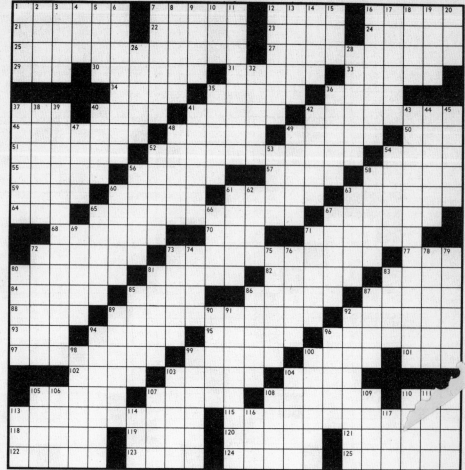

ACROSS

1. Shuns
7. Showers
12. "...falling —— log"
16. Solidifies
21. Mint plant
22. Being led
23. Fasten
24. —— in the dark
25. Song for Pierre
27. Headgear
29. Highest note
30. Mine passages
31. Correct
33. Wartime raider
34. Loose
35. Printer's marks
36. Textile degrees
37. Veterans' org.
40. Diagonal
41. Works
42. Subject of a pop-song ode
46. A chicken —— pot
48. Pouch
49. "—— Now"
50. —— tree
51. Akin
52. Pottery
54. Barbecue rod
55. Hindu temples
56. Bancroft and others
57. Top-notch
58. Pule
59. Otherwise
60. Babble
61. Goes by plane, old style
63. Go pale
64. More: Sp.
65. Large sponge
67. Common contraction
68. Plants of regions
70. Gob
71. Water tank
72. Related
73. Electrical device
77. Physics and others: Abbr.
80. City officials
81. Old-World sandpiper
82. Leaders
83. Black
84. Wells's Mr.

Kipps et al.
85. Part of a Kipling trio
86. Coin
87. View
88. Direction: Fr.
89. Rich and strong
92. Hartebeest
93. Scot's snow
94. Cleaving tools
95. News sections, for short
96. Joined in a way
97. Trellis
99. More plucky
100. Elan
101. First, etc., in football: Abbr.
102. Throw
103. Church part
104. Church season
105. Popular refrain of tots
107. Show off
108. Careened
110. Tangled mass
113. Period of

revelry
115. Collins mystery
118. Lop off
119. 20 quires
120. "—— give you ..."
121. Two-seated wagons
122. Like a fork
123. State: Abbr.
124. Nova Scotian cape
125. U.S. Indians

DOWN

1. Summit
2. African river
3. Other: Sp.
4. Partner of ft.
5. —— Irae
6. Hot-tempered one
7. Moon valleys
8. "What's in ——?"
9. Obsession: Suffix
10. One, two, etc.: Abbr.
11. Like sugar
12. Attacks
13. Mythical deities

14. Discovery
15. Priest's robe
16. Auto-drive part
17. Snoops
18. Mother of Zeus
19. Peace Nobelist in 1946
20. State and Main: Abbr.
26. Southern caverns
28. Be away, as a suburb
32. Turmoil
35. Classifies
36. French drink
37. Crown
38. Writer Thirkell
39. Odd plant
40. $2-window fodder
41. Serving piece
42. Vegetables
43. Houseleek
44. Deems
45. Corroded
47. Farewell: Lat.
48. African people

49. Word after one fell
52. Growing out
53. Japanese island
54. Devon, for one
56. Hungarian hero
58. Pup
60. French dads
61. —— of potatoes
62. Color
63. Caprices
65. Roulette colors
66. Exist: Fr.
67. Sycophant
69. Harold of silents
71. Mont ——
72. Lawrence's "—— Rod"
73. Market sign
74. Therefore
75. Orator
76. S.A. tanagers
78. Swindlers
79. Sam and others
80. Parsonage
81. Planing tool
83. Behold: Lat.
85. Lily plants

86. Parent in London
87. Abel's brother
89. San Quentin
90. Jalopy
91. Fanciful
92. Give ear
94. Nonplused
96. —— -man
98. Adjust
99. Flashes
100. Early explorer of America
103. Opera parts
104. Delineates
105. French mate
106. Vingt- ——
107. Entreaty
108. Scant
109. Certain medals
110. Polish measure
111. Pay up
112. Hardy girl
113. N.Y., for one
114. Chair part
116. Initials of fairy-tale author
117. Chinese pagoda

Word Assortment
by William A. Lewis Jr.

ACROSS

1. Salad plant
6. Interlock
10. Tops
15. Confine
16. Russian country house
17. Up and around
19. Office worker
21. Companionably
23. Vessel
24. Gobs
25. The past
27. Shell-gamer's need
28. Leak
30. Adds up
32. Brother
33. Spoiled one
34. Council
36. Confines
38. Accessible
39. Corresponded
40. Midge
42. Out of shape
44. Prepares vichyssoise
45. Filler material
48. Certain mail
49. At will
50. State: Abbr.
51. Tease
53. Word in L.A.
54. Good word for Charlie Brown
55. Military group: Abbr.
57. Like some containers
59. Redistilled liquor
63. To the good
65. Hope and
66. Roast: Fr.
67. Catch
68. Very unpleasant
70. Marina sights
72. Wax
73. Actor Claude
74. Certain room
75. One's nature
77. Form of Rachel
78. Guzzles
80. Take it easy
82. Kohinoor, e.g.
84. Defend
85. Harbor sound
87. Snow vehicle
88. Car co-ops
89. Livid
90. Catty sound
92. Easy prey
95. Ill temper
96. Skillet
98. Bit of liquor
100. Blue or green
101. Bravo!
102. Academic elite, informally
104. "There —— any more"
106. Hebrew letter
107. Prosperous
109. Military to-dos
112. In a grand manner
113. Roundish
114. French relative of F.B.I.
115. Giggle
116. Indiana port
117. Gambling choice

DOWN

1. Flavor
2. Modern convenience
3. Lazy writer's abbreviation
4. Please
5. Chair part
6. Degrees: Abbr.
7. Nymph of myth
8. Place for things
9. Breadstuff
10. Tavern workers
11. Rice
12. Runners
13. Kind of ear
14. Aerial
15. Digging tools
16. Housecoat
17. Held back
18. Very
20. Support
22. Ship men
26. Reruns
29. Place to fish
31. Rebuff
33. Oral summary
35. Smear
37. Cheerful
39. Companion of deals
41. Former Russian
43. Move heavily
44. Bin
45. Biblical wife
46. Word of greeting
47. Men's-wear items
49. "Across the maneuver
52. Variety acts
54. Early invaders
56. Light covered cart: Var.
58. Feature of an old floor
59. Informal title
60. Provincial
61. Deep sound
62. Joined, in a way
64. Factotums, old style
66. Pay, in a way
69. Uncontrollable
70. Relative of uh-huh
71. Earth fault
74. Ruthless
76. Season
78. Team that scores upsets
—— plain"
79. Scads
80. Car
81. —— bien
83. See 61 Down
84. Violin stroke
85. Word for a pilot
86. Not at all
89. Take offense
91. Tenuous strip
93. Quaker-ladies
94. Meaning
96. Violin item
97. Roman emperor
99. Grind, as teeth
102. Memphian deity
103. Burn
105. Straight
108. Caustic
110. Pen
111. Altar: Lat.

Punny Girls

by John Willig

ACROSS

1. Scheme
6. Gaucho gear
11. Where the Acheron flows
16. Saw
21. Raid
22. "Stop ——"
23. Grownup
24. Parlor piece
25. Gateway to U.S. wonderland?
27. Invalid, in a girlish way
29. Have status
30. Chinese weight
31. Without spirit
33. Eases
34. Seam
35. Catch-all for some
36. "—— forgive…"
37. With venom
41. Film director
42. Bird: Lat.
43. Shield knob
47. Somewhat
48. Police conveyance?
50. Scottish terrier
51. Atoll ingredient
52. Too much: Music
53. —— jacet
54. Golf nickname
55. Periods
56. —— over lightly
57. Father of Boys Town
61. Relative of a plater
62. Rude refusal
63. Entertain
65. Dessert
66. Moving back and forth
68. Just manage, with "out"
69. Going at a good clip?
73. Tax, in Dublin
74. At hand
76. Electric ——
77. Ring name
78. Some lotions
80. Girlish tantrums

82. Fuller explanations?
88. Kipling's O'Hara
91. Former Italian colonial
93. Bishop in "Henry V"
94. Mistreat
95. Feminine suffix
96. Drop bait lightly
97. Small covered passage
100. Annoyer
101. Formerly, of old
102. Part of long-run play title
104. Dawn goddess
105. Split ——
106. Play part
107. Illuminated
108. Settles anew?
111. Withdraw
112. "Simon ——"
113. V.I.P. place
114. Hawk leashes
115. Chiding mother, for one
116. Odd: Scot.
117. Links
118. Kind of collar
119. Basic items
123. Stale
124. Assert
125. Sumptuous
129. Tag for a hot rodder?
131. Name for an eloper?
134. "—— at last!"
135. Siouan
136. Old word of regret
137. Kind of crime
138. Smartly dressed
139. Carried
140. Retreats
141. Stage devices

DOWN

1. Distant
2. Piano hit of 1920's
3. Pluck
4. Duchesse, for one
5. Observe
6. Kind of garden
7. What Buzzards Bay is
8. Asian sea
9. Hamilton bill
10. Signifies
11. Cutting tool
12. Astaire
13. In a proper way
14. Building wing
15. Has top billing
16. Confuse
17. Low place
18. English river
19. Trot or gallop
20. Butts
26. Saragat's country
28. Tidings
32. Lauder, to cockneys
34. Certain tone
35. Paw, in Paris
36. Salad ingredient
37. Creed set up in 325 A.D.
38. Hooded jacket
39. Girl's gift

40. Start of Clement Moore poem
41. Postal device
42. Hillbilly's anti
43. Mideast initials
44. Attired like a mouse
45. Some Irishmen
46. Walk ——
48. Heartsease
49. Eureka's relative
50. Jargon
52. Barnstorm
57. Newspaper section: Abbr.
58. One kind of gift
59. Started, to poets
60. Inert gases
63. Camel's-hair cloth
64. Textile dealer, in London
65. Filch
67. Kind of train: Abbr.

70. Pasture
71. Winglike part
72. Liturgical prayers
75. Reckoned: Abbr.
79. Noun suffix
80. Awards
81. Yemen's land
83. Resinous substance
84. Lack of vigor: Var.
85. —— du Diable
86. Building beams
87. Inning units
89. Where to be on a rainy day
90. One's own thing
92. Grate upon
98. Some turkeys
99. Group of fifty
100. Revolutionary general
101. Of the church: Abbr.
103. Muscle: Suffix

105. Super's helper
106. Long time
108. Sound range
109. Polished
110. Smallest one
111. Disdain
113. Attracted
115. Swiss ——
116. Sec. of State under Cleveland
117. Swell
118. Oust
119. Thai language
120. Honduran port
121. "Thanks ——!"
122. Confined (with "up")
123. —— and potatoes
124. Macaws
125. Young salmon
126. Bone: It.
127. Organ part
128. Gossipy women
130. Inner: Prefix
132. Drink
133. Owned

Down to the Sea
by B.H. Kruse

ACROSS

1. Russian agency
5. Hawaiian shrub
10. Ship of ——
15. Like: Prefix
19. Oriental babysitter
20. Records
21. Ocean routes
22. Pal of void
23. Kind of skirt
24. First ocean steamer
26. Duck
27. Crucial time in tennis
29. Stake
30. Leather workers
32. Armadillos
33. Experience
35. Polish city
36. Reproductive cell
38. Captain's role, at his table
39. Hags
42. Jewish months
43. Famed clipper
46. —— cost
47. Kind of pronoun: Abbr.
48. Hall of ——
49. Blockhead
51. Broadway signs
52. Roof ornament
53. Constitution
55. Least in age: Abbr.
56. Flag
58. German river
59. Macaw
62. Church area
63. One kind of man
65. Auricular
66. New Havenite
67. Socrates, for one
68. Buffoon
72. Fleming
75. Liner holding Atlantic record
79. French article
80. Group
82. Emphatic word after yes or no
83. Attention-calling words
84. Building beam
85. U.S. admiral (1874-1939)
87. Some ads
89. Jewish liturgy
90. Definite period
92. Sugar source
93. Toolbox item
94. Part of a poetic foot
95. Take part in
97. Bake eggs
98. Thugs
100. Town on Thames
101. One who makes trades
104. Within: Prefix
105. Genoese admiral
109. Lion's trademark
110. Sea, to poets
111. Radioman's O.K.
112. Certain exams
113. Tritons
114. Fat
115. Famed acting family
116. Outdated
117. Printer's term

DOWN

1. Perth wear
2. Gallic companion
3. Chris craft
4. Clipper owners
5. Clothes
6. Otto and E.J.
7. In —— (peeved)
8. French article
9. King of Judah
10. Point of view
11. Owner of la plume
12. Bancroft
13. Crumpets' companion
14. Biblical valley
15. Pleads
16. Historic troopship
17. Relating to: Suffix
18. Reverses
25. Shakespeare's "—— deep"
28. Horse fare
31. U.S. bureau
33. One who lugs
34. Houston player
35. Tea
36. Stares
37. Proficient
38. Like N.Y. in summer
39. Aisle walker
40. Genesis name
41. Method: Abbr.
43. Framework
44. Pantywaist
45. Accesses
48. Roman historian
50. Chinese silk
53. Eastern vine
54. Knobby
57. Direction
60. Creeks
61. Do Hamlet
63. Procrastinator's word
64. Writer James and family
65. English impostor
67. Lorelei, for one
68. Swiss city
69. Type of lifeboat
70. Walking ——
71. Slangy word of derision
72. "—— I can do it"
73. Asian range
74. Ill-fated ocean
76. Palms
77. Detection device
78. A title for Macbeth
81. Fulton's Folly
84. Ancient vessels
86. Being, in philosophy
88. Colombian town
89. Came down
91. French wine
93. Group of words
95. Scatter
96. Gardeners
97. Canvas
98. Diamonds
99. Two-toed sloth
100. Keenness
101. Bikini parts
102. ——en point
103. What's left
106. Alternative
107. Afr. brandy
108. Hour: It.

Thanksgiving Fare by W.W.

ACROSS

1. Designation: Abbr.
5. Between sum and fui
9. Tricks
14. Lion
19. Whimpers
21. —— a million
22. Creators of jams
23. Shape in a way
24. Holiday dining décor
27. Plant fiber
28. Columbus campus
29. Get the air
30. Of a body fiber: Prefix
31. Begins to work
32. Limousines
34. Ventured
36. Girl's name
38. Controversial
40. Mom's baking standby
44. Words of disavowal
48. Officer of ——
50. Keen qualities of sense
51. Supporting bar
52. Coty
53. Of a volcano
54. Frolics
55. Young one
58. Airstrips: Abbr.
61. Day times: Abbr.
62. Sandwich filler
63. Football platoon
65. Atelier items
68. C.P.A. job
69. U.S. composer
70. Yearly pay for a few
72. Foulard items
75. Derisive sound
76. Table décor
80. Roman halls
82. Western smokes
84. Social bore
85. Fawn
86. Moslem prayer
87. Dark rock
89. Late-flower-
ing tulip
91. Soup seeds
94. Man's nickname
95. Bone: Prefix
97. Caesar's but
98. City in Picardy
99. Cubes and spheres
102. Hindu deity
104. Behaves well
105. Road menaces
107. Parallel
110. Novelist's problem
111. Sleigh for today's grandma
113. Shooting, in a way
116. Bare the head, old style
118. "It's —— thing"
120. Scourge
121. Scott hero
124. Some dogs
128. Certain Italian, to French
130. Peer Gynt's mother
131. Alert
132. Repast topper
135. Nonconformist
136. Skin: Prefix
137. Ten: Lat.
138. Obtain repairs
139. —— work
140. Tree secretion
141. Biblical tower
142. Scout groups

DOWN

1. Place in proximity
2. Heartbeat control device
3. Strong approval
4. Your: Fr.
5. Inward: Anat.
6. Ocean-research unit
7. One source of salt
8. Kind of service man: Abbr.
9. Prestige
10. Standout
11. Doer: Suffix
12. Subway workers
13. Silence!
14. Hit a high fly
15. Holiday menu item
16. 1969 champs
17. Famed island
18. Arabian Sea gulf
20. Frugal one
21. Scot's alas
25. Privileged people
26. Well-done part of a roast
31. Red or White
33. Residue
35. Verb suffix
37. Possessive
39. Vegetable for mom's table
41. Mayan month
42. News pieces
43. Spanish relatives
45. State: Abbr.
46. Slue
47. "—— deal!"
49. Evergreen
51. Drool
54. Musical ending
55. Sea birds
56. In progress
57. Crux of a holiday meal
59. Kennel sound
60. Ad subject
62. Home-cooked item
63. Metric units: Abbr.
64. Tennis scores, in a way
66. Medit. island
67. Eagles
68. Galatea's beloved
71. Kiln
73. Craft
74. Agreed with
77. Khan
78. Well-known Italian
79. Small violins
81. Scottish county
83. Misfortunes
87. City of Brazil
88. Of an acid
90. Like a moonlit night
91. Bedside item
92. Ludwig
93. Spanish lad
94. Name in movies
96. Refrain syllable
99. Like a freshly cleaned suit
100. Lower
101. Indian titles of respect
103. One who transfers property
105. Scottish
precipitation
106. Slipped over
108. Girl with a headset: Abbr.
109. Veld animal
111. Short of
112. Third of a famous nine
114. Stick one's
115. Welcomes
117. Songs
119. Eastern V.I.P.
121. —— avis
122. Was beholden to
123. Cake
125. Comparative suffixes
126. Prefix for god or john
127. Oxygen prefix
129. Navy V.I.P.: Abbr.
132. New Deal man
133. Presidential initials
134. G-man

Getting the Word
by Jack Luzzatto

ACROSS

1. Dog-sled driver
7. Hard feelings
13. Takes it easy
19. Bird with hanging nest
20. Watcher over me?
21. Specialized ornament
22. Site of S.M.U.
23. Wings of buildings
24. Minimal beach wear
25. Like printers' hands
26. Customarily
28. Wool fabric from Asia
30. Sholokhov's quiet river
31. You: Ger.
32. Woodworkers' aids
33. Dostoevski
34. Glacial offshoot
35. Spoiled-child specialties
37. Water-proofed, as ropes
38. Meticulous
39. Estimate
40. Furthers
41. Place for rolling stock
43. Draw from
46. Deprives of energy
48. System of beliefs
51. Adversary
52. Morose
53. Rage and elation
56. Heels
57. Seafood treat
58. Telling of tomorrow
59. Brief mornings
60. Models of cold perfection
62. Music to a matador
63. Comic's routine
65. Acclaims
66. Amused expression
67. Slipping, as of a disk
68. Slick
69. Vogue
70. Circe's product
71. Movie pioneer
73. Mrs. Grundy and others
74. Hindu scriptures
76. Bungle
77. Blueprint
78. Younger son
81. Crafty qualities
83. Sudden city
87. Hebrew measure
88. Game for anyone
89. Revivers for swooning ladies
90. Tramp, for short
91. Take forcibly
92. Rouse to fury
93. Disconcert
94. Nautical place
95. Numeral system
97. Role for wide-eyed girl
99. Out of the weather
101. Undeveloped
102. Desserts
103. Snows: Fr.
104. Grooms
105. Officer to Macbeth
106. One who manages

DOWN

1. Follower of fashion
2. Muse of astronomy
3. Lustrous
4. Pious
5. High note
6. Strong of purpose
7. Characterizations
8. Encouraging word
9. Trawl
10. Metal fastener
11. Adjective for Podunk
12. Live
13. Pole tossed by Scots
14. Overlook
15. Arctic diver
16. Projector inserts
17. Vocalists
18. Meager
20. Surfeits
27. Show rage
29. Physical entity
32. Slang for easy money
33. Mistaken suppositions
34. Cage bird, for short
36. Crops
37. "—— the tales..."
38. Beer heads
40. Rock salt
42. Takes as one's own
43. Vamoose
44. Charms
45. Colorful Arctic fall
46. Followed
47. Successive
49. Drove
50. Chemical dye
52. Mops of hair
54. Time period
55. Rises on a wave
57. Inclined
58. Edible South Sea worm
60. Earth
61. Berates
64. Twist
66. Wordless sound
68. Cheerfully
69. Mine vehicles
72. Height
73. Novelist's concern
75. Ripe
77. End of the earth
78. Island makers
79. Unaware of right or wrong
80. Douglas forte
82. Some wear, familiarly
83. Military centers
84. Accommodate
85. Expressionless
86. Most recent
88. Diplomatic assets
89. Reject rudely
92. Fur
93. Pearly mussel
94. Saudi Arabian area
96. Nectar collector
98. Dine
100. Born

Gift Suggestions

by Frances Hansen

ACROSS

1. Betty of song et al.
6. Resort in West
11. Makes passes at a fly
18. Wayne and Dix: Abbr.
21. Handy
22. Nasty
23. Narcotic
24. Exclamation
25. Prisoner's castle, in fiction
26. Ice-cream holders
27. Equally taut
28. Ring: Abbr.
29. Words after "Hey" in old song
33. Old British middle class: Abbr.
34. Not public: Abbr.
35. Dickens girl
36. Reddish brown
37. Popular play and movie
44. Razor-blade features
45. "I —— gay musician"
46. Nigerian people
47. Coffee maker
48. Cut off
50. Columbo
51. After Santa
54. "Now, Jonah, he lived in ——"
57. White poplar
59. Eye: Prefix
60. Most like Daddy Warbucks
62. New York town
65. Came onstage
67. Sternward
68. Item for the press
72. In style
75. Nabokov book
76. Superlative endings
79. German spa
81. Raleigh's rival
82. Greatly
84. Something fur me?
87. Specify
88. River to Tiber
89. Quick to learn
90. Summit
91. Cameroon tribe
93. Farm crop
94. Bewildered
96. My gal
98. "—— was worth while..."
101. Start of Nash verse
105. —— orchard (Western grove)
109. Beluga
112. United
113. Smile lasciviously
115. Prepare
116. Italian wine town
117. Upon: Fr.
118. Asian or swine
119. Guevara
121. Bill
122. Iranian money
124. Singer Bailey?
131. Fisherman
133. Peacock blue
134. Islet
135. In addition
136. Familiar Dickens phrase
143. Purpose
144. In fashion
145. Lend ——
146. Mennonite
148. Vital cell acid: Abbr.
149. Ancient one
150. Hawaiian chants
151. Slow to catch on
152. "—— lords aleaping..."
153. Old and New England towns
154. Rub out
155. "King Lear" role

DOWN

1. Kissing kin, familiarly
2. Baby's shoe size
3. Lab burner
4. "—— want a brand-new car"
5. Did a garden job
6. Spore sacs
7. Part of the winter scene
8. Poilu's wine
9. Like Adam's abode
10. ——-ce pas?
11. Tint delicately
12. Felt indisposed
13. Equally high
14. Pronoun
15. Prefix for an Asian
16. Orgs.
17. "—— is cast"
18. Confronting, with "to"
19. Most like Twiggy
20. Sea N.E. of West Indies
30. Squatter's cult
31. Del Sarto
32. O'Casey
37. River to Moselle
38. All: Prefix
39. Secular
40. Emulated Webster
41. Asian tents
42. Hebrew letter
43. Ruby and emerald
49. Marquette
52. "I'll take ——" (coat choice)
53. Of bronze: Abbr.
55. "Scots Wha ——"
56. English poet
57. Landon
58. Kind of nut
61. Corset part
63. Tack
64. Swiss painter
66. Turnpike exit
69. Land mass
70. Delighted
71. Letters
72. Dickens, for short
73. Symbol of satiety
74. Place to wear furs
77. Nordic bard
78. Recipe abbreviation
80. Miserly
83. Turner
85. "—— the bag"
86. Chemical compound
87. Word with cote or tail
89. Totals
92. Wide collar
95. Namesakes of a Spanish queen
97. Ibsen role
99. Son of Odin
100. Ms. men
102. After "days of"
103. "—— summer's day"
104. Between huit and dix
106. To thee: Fr.
107. Now: Lat.
108. Graf ——
109. Widely separated
110. —— with (conforms)
111. Set arranger
114. Solvents
118. Matures
120. Diminutive suffix
123. Opening word
125. In —— position (resting)
126. Armed ship
127. Infer
128. Anglo-Indian troop
129. Hair dressing
130. Lodged
132. Take it easy
137. Tender, Scotch style
138. Fake: Abbr.
139. Specify
140. Gds.
141. Tweed's group
142. She: It.
147. Part of H.R.H.

On Location

ACROSS

1. Upstairs and downstairs
6. California wine valley
10. Drooping
14. Change lines in music
19. Map addition
20. Civil War combatants
22. U.S. textile inventor
23. Cobbler
24. Air terminal of sorts
26. Plow soles
28. Word of obligation
29. Mythical place of darkness
30. Hankering
31. Basilica area
33. Periodical, for short
34. Minuscule
35. Compass reading
36. Resign
38. Mischief-maker
40. McGuffey's output
43. Gyrated
45. Coated iron plates
47. "—— blue?"
48. Where Ybor City is
52. Look after
53. Locations
54. Business-letter abbreviation
55. Wind around
56. "...can you spare ——?"
58. Recipients
61. Bulrush
62. Went on about
63. Sunday talk: Abbr.
64. Butterfly
66. Home of the IRT
67. Weak consonants
69. Belief
71. Some jewelry
73. Expose
74. Fur animal
77. Mauna ——
80. Restraint
82. "Recessional" word
84. Nickname for Australians
86. Couple
87. Kilmer title
89. Relatives of rabbets
90. TV name
92. Precipitated, old style
93. Item in the black
94. "—— was saying"
95. Worthless
96. Gets off the track
97. Dour
99. Before
100. ——-terre
102. Dull noise
105. German article
106. High note
108. Insulative material
109. Freudian concepts
112. Hill nymphs
114. Orange oil
117. Tragus
119. Certain go-between
123. Flycatcher
124. Drew, for one
125. Palmist's reading
126. Equip for battle, old style
127. River to Hudson Bay
128. Paris airport
129. Whilom
130. Eye swellings: Var.

DOWN

1. Little girl
2. Lizard genus
3. Galaxies
4. Scout doing
5. Rill
6. Filch
7. Stein's repetition
8. Robin's pal
9. —— Domini
10. Old Greek war cry
11. Certain U.S. campus
12. Like three
13. Before omega
14. Welcomes again
15. Let up
16. Payola
17. High male voice
18. Dodger name
21. Masses
25. Urgency
27. Barbecue parts
32. Escarpments
34. Professional mourner
37. Bones et al.
38. Kind of flight
39. Hodge-podge
41. Mike man
42. In a brown study
43. Movie biggie
44. Foot keyboards
46. Kind of book
49. Funicular
50. Synthetic fiber base
51. Man's nickname
54. Arthurian lady
57. German river
59. Happening
60. Singing voice: Abbr.
65. Asian boundary river
68. Cul-de- ——
70. Singer Diana
72. Got the import
73. Can. province
75. Pinkish colors
76. Oil jar
78. Soup pods: Var.
79. Slanting
81. Axes
83. Starting places
85. People of Assam
88. Certain watchmakers
91. Roman official
95. —— -hand
98. Girl
101. Storehouses
102. Famed Idaho name
103. Tropical palm
104. Thought-provoking
107. Skeptical
108. Mickey et al.
110. U.S. industrialist: 1804-1886
111. Banana bunches
113. Lily plant
115. Eye
116. Learning: Scot.
118. Let out
120. Even if, for short
121. Chalice veil
122. Asian holiday

Yuletide Thoughts

by Anne Fox

ACROSS

1. —— Flow
6. Give up
10. Erst
16. Kind of tree
20. Cry ——
21. "Render therefore —— Caesar . . ."
22. Greek goddess
23. U.S. statesman
25. Of a bone
26. Nobility: Ger.
27. Type of patch
28. Exciting edition
29. State: Abbr.
30. Give the once-over
32. Go up
34. Pourboire
36. Gen. Arnold
37. Conniption
39. A lot
40. Marrow
41. Saison
42. Fatima slept here
43. Savor
45. Panegyric
46. Gloomy one
47. Words by John Donne
53. Famous hunter
54. Egg: Prefix
55. Plain of southwest U.S.
56. Old English letter
57. Soak
58. Mudskippers
61. —— majesty
62. Categorizes
66. Aleutian island
68. Whimsical
70. One of a Latin trio
72. Spelt
73. Sub follower
75. L.B.J. in-law
77. Kind of coffee
79. Wing
80. Words by Walter de la Mare
87. —— polloi
88. Out of the way
89. Relative of esse
90. Outer: Prefix
91. Old Greek coins
93. Duration
95. Harangue
98. Foil
102. Might
104. Passport entry
106. Asian area
108. Tiergarten sight
109. A degree
110. Capricious
112. Smidgen
113. Dutch wife
115. Words by Esther S. Buckwalter
121. Widely
122. Waters: Lat.
123. Christmas
124. Writer Rand
125. Relative of st.
126. Chinese tree
127. English age: Abbr.
128. Alsatian brandy
132. Marble
133. Drink
134. Ruled out
137. Channels
138. Live
139. Yeah
141. Links
143. Approach
145. Ruy Diaz de Bivar
147. American pioneer
148. Republic created in 1948
149. System of exercises
150. Like some seals
151. Weather word
152. Hoss
153. Bustle
154. African lake

DOWN

1. Work group
2. Arum lily
3. Birdlike
4. Grass genus
5. Following "The Gospel"
6. Scruple
7. Wavy, in heraldry
8. Native: Suffix
9. See 62
10. Words from St. Luke
11. Living
12. Holy picture
13. Come to earth
14. Siouan
15. Speak of
16. Words by William Morris
17. Relative of a whammy
18. Busy
19. Corrigendum
24. Micronesian native
31. Pacific island
33. Rabbit tails
35. "It grows as ——" (N. Mex. motto)
38. Call to hunting dogs
39. Forte
40. Defendant's answer
43. French painter
44. Game piece
45. Native
47. Roman public areas
48. State: Abbr.
49. Hayworth
50. Raise ——
51. U.S. agency
52. Exclamation of surprise
59. Puts out
60. ". . . and they were —— afraid"
62. With 9 Down, words from Ecclesiastes
63. Pipe
64. High
65. Manche capital
67. Prefix with corn or cycle
69. Letter sign-off
71. African people
74. Friendliness
76. Impetus
78. Board member: Abbr.
80. Cut up
81. Tramp
82. Kind of act
83. Drink
84. Canadian writer
85. Sew together
86. In our time
92. Focusing medium
94. State: Abbr.
96. Persian rug
97. Literature Nobelist in 1948
99. Sea of Russia
100. Rounder
101. Go to ——
103. Each: Fr.
105. Sports gear
107. Air: Abbr.
110. Part of a taxi meter
111. Caesar, at one time
114. Bombast
115. Swift's "Tale ——"
116. Blankets
117. Samuel Butler novel
118. Kind of fringe
119. "—— child is loving . . ."
120. —— monde
128. Sheikdom of Arabia
129. Holy: Lat.
130. Blubbers
131. Gabler
134. Exceedingly
135. Son of Isaac
136. Calendar abbreviation
137. Academy Award film: 1958
140. Spanish number
142. "A rose —— . . ."
144. Dash's partner
146. Put down

Gadget Counter

by William Lutwiniak

ACROSS

1. Rebuff
5. Complies
10. Ululates
14. —— song
18. Girl who wants, and gets
19. Musical piece
20. Lively dance
21. Porthos et Aramis
22. Surprise
25. Platform
26. Caprices
27. Points
28. Clefts
30. Neighbor of Ala.
31. Cocktail garnishes
32. Noun ending
33. Calling by name
36. Tonsorial service
37. Self-inflated one
41. Have —— to
42. Manicurist's concern
44. ——-disant
45. Italian numeral
46. Bearish times
47. Coffee-makers
48. Esteemed panfish
49. Numerical prefix
50. Honestly
54. Folkways
55. Guards
57. Fencing move
58. Of a cereal
59. Incites
60. Small cabaret
61. Toxophilite gear
62. Wrap
63. Land of Minos
64. Encircled, of old
67. Money of Thailand
68. Contributes
70. Galena
71. Wishes undone
72. Reward, old style
73. Have a go
74. Silk, in Paris
75. Neighbor of Oreg.
76. Approached a solution
80. Traveled, in a way
81. Combinations
83. Staff men
84. Compulsion
85. Over-eager
86. Villain's forte
87. The McCoy: Abbr.
88. New York
91. City of Peru
92. Certain writers
96. His: Fr.
97. Performs obsequies of a kind
100. Popular garnish
101. —— price
102. Kind of seal
103. Topnotch
104. Berra
105. Social group
106. Service-women
107. For fear that

DOWN

1. European
2. She-wolf: Sp.
3. Sleep like ——
4. Hill of Rome
5. Near future
6. Part of a White House name
7. Individuals
8. Sound of gusto
9. Background
10. Inexperienced ones
11. "—— well"
12. Pronoun
13. TV offerings
14. Withering
15. Straw in the wind
16. Haystack
17. Invites
20. Term in grammar
23. Vogue
24. Turning point
29. Farm animals
31. Washer cycle
32. Group of three
33. What Sam made too long
34. Con ——, in music
35. Firing
36. Sounds of dolor
37. Granite center
38. Daft
39. City on the Seine
40. Pointers
42. Atropos et al.
43. Cloud: Fr.
46. Nasty
48. Relative of tequila
50. Exams
51. Blackthorn fruit
52. S.A. capital
53. Below: Ger.
54. Corday's victim
56. Street sounds
58. One lap, for Armstrong
60. City on the Mark
61. Boundary
62. —— Arabia
63. Collegians
64. Men of Tartu: Abbr.
65. Iroquoians
66. Realty papers
67. Hat feature
68. Covered with moisture
69. Athirst
72. Musical instruments
74. Of a branch of medicine
76. Fiji's capital
77. Bert of golf
78. Mortgages
79. Conceives
80. What Jack did
82. Papeete's island
84. Wood nymphs
86. Revered one
87. Different
88. Like last week's meat
89. Melange
90. Oil used in varnish
91. Igneous rock
92. Immunologist's concerns
93. Oxford
94. Sawbucks
95. Opposite of dele
98. Shoshonean
99. Fortune

Word Collection
by Lewis C. Breaker

ACROSS

1. Note holders: Abbr.
4. Libations
8. Bring bad luck
12. French soul
15. Mortar ingredient
17. Two
20. Comminuted
21. Inducting
23. Eats greedily
24. Light-bulb filler
26. Kind of ale
27. Prevent
28. Silvery
32. Former Indian state
33. Towel lettering
34. Excursion
35. Beauty of myth
37. Shreds
38. "Wherefore —— thou?"
39. Grates
40. Scattering
42. Method: Abbr.
43. Ferment
44. Handled rudely
45. Weaving frame
47. Hetty and Lorne
50. Machetes
51. Green gem minerals
55. Take it easy
56. Spartan serf
57. Origination
58. Son of Adam
59. Surrounding spaces
61. Asiatic river
62. Donkey disciples
64. Certain stocks
65. Belief
66. Slides
67. Learns, old style
68. Propositions
69. Examine critically
70. Turns over
71. Japanese assembly
72. U.S. air group: Abbr.
75. Mean persons
77. Middle East waterway
78. German article
81. Moslem holy man
83. —— the punch
84. Raced
85. Spanish muralist
86. Edible roots
88. Assets
90. Legal thing
91. Bouquet de Flore
93. Channel seaweed
94. Stock exchange man
95. Payment
99. Place of suffering
101. A judge, at times
102. Put in ecstasy
103. Astral sign
104. Throw
105. Bunch of bananas
106. Road curve

DOWN

1. Conduit under a road
2. New York's North and East
3. Inkling
4. —— Baba
5. Skink, gecko, et al.
6. Issue
7. Grasslike plant
8. Estate tenures for wives
9. Cheshire Cheese, for one
10. Steel town in Norway
11. Indian memorial
12. Extemporize
13. Liliom's creator
14. Posers
15. Trill
16. European coins: Abbr.
18. Shrew
19. Vitality
20. City on Vltava River
22. German author
25. Sergeant's words
28. Yorkshire river
29. Angered
30. "—— or never!"
31. Removes hair
34. L.A. team
36. Electrodes
39. Wryneck genus
40. Name for Shropshire
41. One using an exit
43. Intense ones
44. Greek state
46. Muezzin's perch
47. Alumni, for short
48. Establishment opposer
49. Varnish ingredient
50. Lahr and others
51. Locks up
52. Eras
53. Musical work
54. Aegean island
56. Warmer
57. Snoops
59. Modern home construction
60. Nobles
63. Smart
65. In the home of: Fr.
67. Post-Thanksgiving menu
68. One-all
70. Small violins
71. Union obligation
72. Hindu guitar
73. Bewilders
74. Kind of sundae
76. Menlo Park monogram
77. Apparition
78. Eastern cedars
79. M. Lupin
80. Metric measure
82. Illinois city
84. Knowing, old style
85. Private eye
87. Free-for-all
89. Fads
90. Minotaur's home
92. Greek goddess of vengeance
94. Recipe abbreviation
96. Opposite of syn.
97. Army man: Abbr.
98. French adjective
100. Actor of sorts

New Year's Party

by Frances Hansen

ACROSS

1. Order to torpedoman
6. Present
11. "—— are about to die..."
16. Architect Jones
21. Word games: Abbr.
22. Of an acid group
23. French airmail word
24. "Sing —— songs..."
25. —— bell
26. All set
27. Loud cries
28. Hartebeest
29. Broadway phrase
32. "—— fairer than the day"
33. Start of Keats poem
34. Writer Rand
35. Times of day, for short
36. Fervent plea, with "us"
38. Gray: Fr.
40. Collected writings
41. Overseas address
42. Mouth: Slang
43. Sandburg words, after "I am"
52. Sound: Prefix
53. Clement and Marianne
54. Eastern nurse
55. —— good turn
56. The Bulbul Amir
58. Chinese dynasty
59. Nevada bandit
61. Talking bird
65. Decorate again
67. Frown
69. Moves furtively
71. Unit of loudness
72. Zambales people
74. Showy perennials
76. Malay hysteria
78. Sympathy's partner
79. Poe's lament
85. Presidential nickname
86. Famous fiddler
87. Israeli dances
88. Man for introductions
89. Combine: Suffix
91. Fiber plant
94. Xmas V.I.P.
96. Poem part
99. Mustapha Kemal
101. Latecomer's penalty
103. Holiday months: Abbr.
105. Kills
106. Corrode
108. Garish sign
109. Ascended rapidly
111. Intentions
112. What "no man lives without"
118. Bread: Prefix
119. Greek letters
120. "Ain't We Got ——?"
121. Savvy remark
122. Part of winter lawn scene
124. Hair job, for short
126. Between sine and non
129. Start of Xmas carol
133. Swords
134. Biblical quotation
137. Alentejo's capital
138. Writer Jones
139. Devil
140. "—— ears," said the rabbit
141. Mortise partner
142. Voter
143. Churchill gesture
144. Titter
145. Cunning
146. Sits
147. Heaps
148. U.S. Indians

DOWN

1. Native of area of Iran
2. J.F.K. and L.B.J.: Abbr.
3. —— check (hunting term)
4. Party worker of a kind
5. Man's name
6. Mountain lake
7. Last in a series
8. Pepys' pride
9. Append
10. Toy
11. "—— with a maid"
12. Consequence
13. Rogers and others
14. One kind of smoke
15. Cricket sides
16. Signed in a way
17. Hostess's oversight
18. "No man —— to his valet"
19. Hunting code
20. Harem room
30. Dialect
31. Heavy hair
32. Shouted down
36. Unit of fuel use: Abbr.
37. Shipping term: Abbr.
39. Catch sight of
40. Pleased sounds
41. Excited
43. Ivan, for one
44. —— Sound, Fla.
45. Tippy furniture
46. Profit's partner
47. Norse king
48. Voice parts
49. Cockney flats
50. False god
51. Funny show: Abbr.
57. Discovered by chance
59. "... —— that I know is damn'd"
60. Union general
62. Result of being trod on
63. "—— Year's gift..."
64. Cure
66. Creates
68. Accompanying
70. Flower stalks
73. Canary's cousin
75. Body fluids
77. Old ones: Abbr.
79. "—— o' kindness"
80. —— -kiri
81. Party disappointment
82. Mahatma
83. Bone: Suffix
84. "Don't ——" (plea of hostess)
90. Label for a gay party, with "Babel"
92. On the ocean
93. Uris
95. Emoting: Abbr.
97. Ferment
98. Set a value on: Abbr.
100. Indian dye
102. "The flowers ——..."
104. Wheat of India
107. Actress Louise et al.
109. Japanese coin
110. Place firmly
112. An Apostle: Abbr.
113. After "now"
114. —— dime
115. Hebrew letter
116. Demote: Colloq.
117. Descendant of Adam's son
123. Intended
124. Tree genus
125. French school
126. Seemingly
127. Up to
128. Equally old, with "of"
130. Madagascan lemur
131. Free-for-all
132. Gardner's namesakes
134. "... see my stuff"
135. Hostess initials
136. Danube tributary
137. King of Siam's word: Abbr.
138. Seat of a sort

Word Parade

by Joseph LaFauci

ACROSS

1. Light gray
9. Slovenly chap
13. Brown, rainbow, etc.
19. Italian cheese
20. Etna's output
21. Greet, as a villain
22. Honor
23. Caused to see red
24. Belong
25. Rhone tributary
26. Unkempt hair
27. Housewifely chore
29. Sourdough's find
30. Yard and boom support
31. Fundamental
33. Girl Friday's station
34. Biblical city
35. Generation
36. With: It.
37. Intolerantly petty
41. Pretends
43. Disapproving sounds
44. Track supports
45. Yesterday, in Rheims
47. Run on
48. Sindbad's bird
49. Never: Ger.
52. Role in "Private Lives"
54. Mechlin or Honiton
55. Serenade, for one
57. Football fields, for short
58. Blackbeard
60. Blend
61. Hollow sound
62. Buffalo of India
63. Epithet for a kettle
64. Gradual decrease
65. —— fixe
66. —— one's time
67. Origin
68. Manservant
69. Crossed out
70. Seize
72. Masonry creation
73. Shopped
75. Name for a dog
76. Hasten
77. Orchestra strings
78. Flying prefix
79. Heraldic fur
81. Big name in Pittsburgh
82. Printed matter
86. Resourceful
88. Face: Slang
89. Hindu deity
90. France's Le ——
91. Cure of a kind
92. Attempt
94. Destiny
95. Days of yore
96. TV comedy star
99. Drone
100. Novarro
101. Wild golf strokes
103. Ancient Syria
104. Working
106. Lease signer
107. Bare
108. Consigned to obscurity
109. Aspects
110. Garden
111. Lee's horse

DOWN

1. Foreshadow
2. Tennis term
3. Ward off
4. Lacerated
5. Corse, for one
6. Ungentlemanly one
7. Cooper Indian
8. Town hall, for one
9. Drifted
10. Byron poem
11. Exaggerated
12. Fast traveler
13. Mull
14. Sonority
15. Kirghiz city
16. Make a wise judgment
17. Defiled
18. Bullock
19. Original
28. Doctrine
31. Filleted
32. Galleon
34. "Fables in Slang" author
36. Numismatist's goodies
38. Freshwater fish
39. Consider
40. Pleasing
42. Like some fast deals
46. Resembling a pest
48. Egyptian city
50. Poor
51. Incited, with "on"
52. Succeed
53. Quality of some psychedelic drugs
55. Actress Velez
56. Watched jealously
57. Eva
59. Alleviate
60. Not making the grade
63. Expert advisers
64. Words for a summer drink
68. Italian actress
69. Singer Bobby
71. Pronoun
72. TV maestro
74. Kind of race
77. Concentrated
80. Feminine suffix
81. Entitle improperly
83. Human being
84. Recover from
85. Tied
86. Degraded
87. "Leave —— to Heaven"
88. Girl's name
90. D.C. hostess
93. Dandy
94. Ruinous
96. Part of N.B.
97. Counterweight
98. Govt. agents
100. Frenzy
102. Coolidge
105. Gun an engine

Centerpieces

by Thomas W. Schier

ACROSS

1. Dolmans
6. Bridge over Moslem hell
11. Climb
16. One at ——
21. Style of painting
22. Employed
23. Ambitious
24. Boo-boo
25. Statesman and author
28. Alpaca's cousin
29. Vaudeville turns
30. Long-billed bird
31. Wide-awake
32. Bullets, in France
33. French marshal
34. More reasonable
35. —— barrel
36. Small antelope
37. Arias
38. Actor
39. Boring tool
40. Orator and novelist
46. L.P., for one
49. New World capital
50. Lear's daughter
51. Greek region
52. Barton
54. Inter ——
55. Darling: It.
56. Military groups
57. Man of parts
58. Bad guy and film bad guy
63. Red
64. Carney
65. Transports
66. Man's name
67. More gentle
68. Antisocial one
69. —— polloi
70. Flower, in Berlin
71. Hallows
74. All rose —— man
76. Use one's neck
77. Houston
80. Canadian city
81. Former quarterback and novelist
84. Cay
85. Sudden reaction
86. Bowling alley
87. River to Baltic
88. Electron tube
89. Song refrain
90. Juvenile writer Oliver
92. Doctor's allotment
94. Telepathy's relative
95. Justice and Ohio man
98. African tribe
100. Effects
101. Highest point
102. Able, Baker, ——
105. Like a swamp
107. —— de lune
109. Cry of contempt
112. Stassen
113. Prospector's companion
114. Dissertation
115. —— War
116. Range areas
117. Socialist and novelist
120. Wrathful
121. Endeavored
122. Kitchen implement
123. Play backer
124. Lease anew
125. Scowl
126. Bergen's Mortimer
127. Solan and gannet

DOWN

1. Broadway name
2. Swiftly
3. —— line
4. Slips
5. Augean stable, for one
6. Alluring
7. Accustom
8. Kind of monger
9. Slippery —— eel
10. Lacrosse team
11. Fur-hunting
12. Frisk
13. Athens sight
14. Baltic native
15. Poetic word
16. Excited
17. German dramatist
18. Wholly
19. Baltic port
20. Take out
26. Muse of comedy
27. Grotto
32. Purses
34. Arrange
35. O'Neill
36. Surmise
37. Old porticoes
38. French painter
39. Understanding
40. Boatman
41. Assess for a purpose
42. "Instant Replay" author
43. —— how
44. Lind or wren
45. Hostile
46. Furious
47. Uneven
48. Do a banquet job
49. —— California
52. Part of a table setting
53. Greene of TV
55. Examples
56. More hostile
59. Hard rubber
60. Small ruling group
61. Collusion
62. Accompanying
63. Stuck to
67. Censure
68. Organized, with "up"
70. Tributary
71. Digression
72. Patriarchs
73. Ship's deck
74. To any degree
75. Kind of poll
76. Kind of gang
77. Type of car
78. Lay
79. Bare
81. City in Japan
82. —— ego
83. Red dye
85. Grayish color
90. Famous trail
91. Implore
92. Legal rights
93. Repute
95. Bagnold
96. Build up
97. Sumac plant
98. "Jane Eyre" creator
99. Ready
102. Church area
103. French port
104. Of a surface
105. Mandalay's land
106. Abalone
107. Italian philosopher
108. Like some excuses
109. Harbor sight
110. 4,500-mile range
111. Games man
113. Do eggs
114. Unconvincing
115. Long hair
117. Badger
118. Corp. officers
119. Witch

The Face Is Familiar

by Eugene T. Maleska

ACROSS

1. Termagant
6. Cleft
12. Epithet for Samuel Johnson
16. Relative of hi-fi
17. Panay port
18. Papa Bear of football
20. Patti Page
22. Wards off
24. Bittern
25. Eating places
26. Bishop's headdress
28. Novelist Levin
29. Grub
30. Entanglement
31. Bremen's river
32. Connery
33. Harriman's nickname
34. Arctic base
35. —— Devi, Indian peak
36. Piece of gossip
37. Schnauzers
39. Mexican shawl
40. Hindu's fast to get justice
41. "—— Lynne"
42. Kyle or Tobin
43. "—— My Sunshine"
45. Play the siren
48. Valuable tree of N.Z.
50. Checks
53. —— Kabaivanska, soprano
54. Rathbone
55. Chilean export
57. Use a straw
58. Useless
59. Cyd Charisse
61. Color in French flag
62. Culbertson
63. Shaman
64. Sniggler
65. Blossom in Brest
66. Prof's stand
68. Wailed
70. Drinks noisily
71. Smuts's philosophy
73. Auction word
74. Korean statesman
75. Iosif V. Dzhugashvili
77. Choir voices
79. Knight fights
83. California's Santa ——
84. Pigtail
85. Cluster
86. Cargo unit
87. Grampuses
88. La ——, Honduran port
89. Fissure
90. "—— move on!"
91. Bowl call
92. Count Basie plays it
93. Cathay
94. Braid of gold or silver
95. Small-time
97. Cary Grant
100. Usher's beat
101. Jeer at
102. Emissary
103. Capitol Hill count
104. Worked on galleys
105. Wroth

DOWN

1. Track official
2. Mackerel-like fish
3. Algerian port
4. Author of "The King Ranch"
5. Ken Murray
6. Nonsense!
7. Agalloch
8. Has an oar-deal
9. Sesame
10. Krypton, for one
11. Miss von Kappelhoff
12. Trout
13. Engage in
14. Drink
15. Leila Koerber
16. "The ravel'd —— of care"
19. Tune
20. Flimflam
21. Name for a ship's carpenter
23. Kringle
27. Congou
30. Anagram for "sheet"
31. Baseball's Big or Little Poison
32. Delusion's partner
34. Royal adornment
35. Natasha Gurdin
36. Midwest airport
38. Meet, as alumni
39. Central theme
40. Indian millet
42. Bed of flowers
44. Horse opera
45. Caliban's opposite
46. Chef's spoon
47. Claudette Colbert
48. Narrative
49. Walked
51. Traffic jam
52. Rail sidetracks
54. George —— (Nathan Birnbaum)
56. "—— Three Lives"
59. City in N.W. Italy
60. Actress Gwyn and others
61. Cornflower
63. Girl in "As You Like It"
65. Hosiery color
67. Turnpike fees
69. Old port of Rome
70. Oyster shell
72. Enriching brine
74. Pope John XXIII
75. Recreation
76. Pacific battle site: 1943
78. Drudged
79. Tia
80. Battologize
81. Announcement
82. Grind together
84. Lillie
85. Suborned
88. Adduces
89. Reprove
90. Alexander's epithet
92. Like thick rugs
93. Voucher
94. Former queen of Greece
96. Dan Beard's org.
98. Dernier
99. Article in Berlin

1

```
COILS    DARKS    ABASH
PICNIC   INANE    FORGOT
SEVENTHHEAVEN     FRITTER
ALIAS  OUT  EASTEND    LEE
KILN   COMES   DEICE   CITE
EOS   SALUTES   OFT   PANED
SNEAKS   SIGNOFF   PINERY
  RAISE    COACH    SOLI
TOVARICH  SITUATIONISM
ABA  RUSES  LEMMA  TEMPO
BONA  STACK  TOOLS  SPAR
ULTRA  ARRAY  RULED  ORE
SISTERSTATES   RECESSES
  WRAY   TILLS   DUMAS
UPTOIT  ICELAND  REGINA
SHARE  ASH  SNOOZES  BAR
HANK  CLIPS  TOROS  FIVE
EST  PULSATE  PIU  ALLIN
REROUTE  PEACEANDQUIET
  DUBLIN  ENTER  DAUNTS
  MILES   ROSES   SHAKY
```

2

```
NOTHIN     BUSHER     BARDS
TARRING   SALTINE   PARTIES
ORIENTS   CLAUDIA   ATACAMA
PRO  CHORAL  BEGGARED  GAR
HALT  ENOLA  SMALL  ALONG
ATEUP  EEDSRE  ANTA  ANTE
TESTED  SETOFF  SAY  TWAIN
ONES  DETOUR  REAR  LCT
TURNUPS   DARTED   DIET
MARS  TACT  SMITES  MARAUD
AGA  HAHA  ILONA  EDIRNE
NONE  UNREGENERATED  MIDI
ORISON  PRONG  TREE  SIS
FEASTS  SONTAG  YELL  SENT
  ATES   DIESES   NEOCENE
ICE  EWES  CRONES  DOUR
TAMAR  GPS  STRAIT  TROPES
ALEM  MEAD  HERPEO  BURNT
LENIS  EAGER  CHIPS  SEGO
IND  TINKERER  HOLLOS  CIA
ADAMANT  NINETEN  ELEMENT
NATIVES  EVADERS  STRIPES
RENEE     SENSES     HABITS
```

3

```
BOGS   COLOR   WRAP   ASST
EXAM   ARISE   HALO   ATETE
AUTUMNALEQUINOX    STEED
USE  ONLY  UNTIE  STUMPS
   NOES   MECHS   CAEN
KAFIRS   BASLE   ALFRESCO
ADAMS   WINTERGREEN   ULM
BULB  LAGO  AGAS  SMEE
OWL  OUTOFSEASON  TOMAN
BASSINET   LAMPS   FAMERS
  BONER   WAGES   BOXER
CHALKS  TOKEN  DANISHES
RACES  SOMERSAULTS  ONA
INKS  SAXE  BEES  BUTS
MOO  SPRINGFIELD  RISES
PINDARIC  RENTS  CELERY
  ALAS   SALAS   SOCK
BOUNTY  SETON  AQUA  FAN
OUNCE   SPRINGASURPRISE
ACTED  TURF  EXEAT  AXIS
THOS   ADAY   READS   JEST
```

4

```
METAL   COSTA   DELAY   STAEL
OZONE   OPTED   EROSE   PORTE
BRONXCHEERS   CROSSBOWMAN
YALE  LENIN  PLANT  LIESTO
   BARON   MEANY   SALA
FASTENER   LEAST   ANDERSON
AMIENS  LIARS  ACIER  ENA
MALAE  WHISTLESTOPS  ACES
IDEST  OASTS  ERRS  TROIS
NINE  TOILE  PATEN  BRENDA
EST  FALLENARCHES  LANDAU
  BLIP     LEE     IDAS
EQUINE  RUBBERBRIDGE  TAA
SUTTER  ASIAN  LURCH  MONT
POLES  AGAS  FOCAL  SARTO
ITER  STAGECOACHES  COIRS
EER  MESNE  ALIKE  PAREUS
DESPISED  STIRS  CHARISMA
  ASTA   TAHOE   DROSS
MALICE  CHIOS  LOATH  XRAY
INANUTSHELL   DUMBWAITERS
LAVIE  AIMEE  ARUBA  BRICE
EMEND  GRADS  WESER  NADIR
```

5

```
SPARED  ALMOST   PASTAS
CAREER  NEEDLER  UNIATE
ORGANA  ARMOIRE  RODMEN
ROAM MANN REGALIA MAS
ELL EASIER RIVET DUSE
DEIGN KAREL VENALIZES
   ACMES  CERE  SNUG
SOLOED CATER ICINGS
REPAID SOPHISTICATION
ADA LOCUM ANARK NACRE
VALE COOPERATION LOGE
ATILT AMANG IONIC BOZ
GENERALISSIMOS CABANE
EREMIC SUZAN TENORS
  EMUS  BEET  PAROL
REINSTATE STERN NOTCH
AUNT ETHAN EVOKES RAE
IRA SNEERED AWAY LIMA
NORATE MIRACLE RIOTER
EPURES ENVIOUS INSERT
DETERS GESTES ESTRAY
```

6

```
EDWARDS ACED FEAR ARTS
LEERIER HOMEPLACE TEHEE
IWEEPFORADONAISHEISDEAD
CASAS ABET STEEDS ARMS
ILL PAYSRENT IMINE
TIETIES REAMOUT STILE
EARTHINESS ANTECESSOR
SAKES EMIT THREADS APE
ARIL APOGEE AGAG
LET SUES ERRANTS AGARS
TOCSINS CATS GOAT BEREA
ELONGATIONS REPRIMANDED
RAWIN OLIO DORE PORTEND
SERGE PANNIER REBS NAL
ISTO CAYUGA RICE
AWN SHIPPED KEPI LUNTS
PATRICIDES SWEETTOOTH
TRIES GALATEA ESTHETE
MATCH RASSLERS RAT
PIRL ATEASE TEER ASFIT
FLOWERINTHECRANNIEDWALL
CLUES DOMINEERS TREACLE
ESTE ELON ELSE SANTEES
```

7

```
ABJURE JANIS SATI NEB
LEASTS EVERT FACILE ONO
EMCEES JACKINTHEBOX PGS
COKE HUSK LOCATE TELIC
TAB POINT BLT ROT OLAN
ONEHORSE SAMARA ALLYE
NIMB PICARESQUE AMES
SIPPED ERINYS UPDO ARA
LAMP DADOES UPAS BAKED
ARBOR LINN BALED ISLED
IAL AAMS STILTS HOCKS
CHEAPJACK ULT OFONESJIB
JAPAN NOBLES ORAN ADE
CAROM BONES HERS ENCLS
PACER TAXI HISSES OKES
ARK TOIT OSIERS DALLAS
ROBE JOHNNYCAKE DUAD
LEVIS OSLERS QUIDNUNC
IQED SES VLS MURES LAR
INUSE PATRIA MEAN ALTA
MII EVERYMANJACK GAMBIT
PAC STALLS DUNCE REMOVE
INK SKYE STEAD STAYED
```

8

```
EBOLI CODED AGES DESK
LENIN AWARE DAMP RITE
LETME TARASBULBA KRON
ACHE CORKSCREW SCIENT
HERTZ LESE AAMILNE
GISARMES GUYS ODI
SORCERIES SUN PANACHE
TREK SPA CHEMIST ROED
IDEST IDOLATER MAENAD
RON ONE CUM SABOT SLY
MUNSTERCHEESE
UME BRICA OPE ATS MBL
NERVES AVOCADOS TIARA
USIA ENRANKS CTO NYET
MANMADE RES THEMAJORS
APL SPYS DESPOTIC
SCIOLTO HEEL REGLE
STEREO POORCLARE TINT
IOOI ULSTERETTE DINAH
OPUS GOUT INHOT AMICI
NASH HYPO STEMS SECTS
```

9

```
MERGE · · ACT · AZOV · GBSHAW
GAMARI · RAH · NAME · NOTATE
EXODERM · GREENCORMORANTS
TITAN · EAU · ACI · ODDMANOUT
EMERALDFEATHER · ASET
MSS · DIET · NEO · EAN · DEBASE
· VITA · MER · CENTS · SONIA
LOINS · PUN · ADDIOS · WILT
CYCLE · DESTAEL · SQUEALSON
ICAL · PORT · BALLOU · AVIESO
DELAMARES · DROP · ELLEN
SEAGATE · PILUS · AIRGAPS
EYING · LCIS · TURNSGRAY
GORGON · RAFAEL · OLEG · RIPE
OVERRATES · TRYOUTS · LEAPS
OUSE · SEETHE · MRS · POESY
PLIED · SNEAD · PAS · LUNN
SENNET · GRD · MUN · BERG · PRI
LIMA · JACKINTHEGREEN
CREDITORS · BCE · OSA · RILLE
PEREGRINEPICKLE · REENTER
APACHE · EMIT · AIL · REGENT
SPLATS · TINE · STS · SNORT
```

10

```
AMPLE · SILK · HEEPS · RIPSAW
KORAN · PLAN · ONTAP · EMOTER
HOOTCHIECOOTCHIE · MALADE
HEAD · ETAT · DEROGATES
RAHS · SEA · HEPTA · EVEREST
ENE · HURLYBURLY · SPAS
DELLAS · POR · APPEAL · CHEM
SATIRE · HOITYTOITY · HOERS
REDUST · NEE · NAS · UVEAS
ROM · HODGEPODGE · GREB
BOSNS · OWE · SRO · VERTIGO
OAK · COUNTER · BELLAMY · EON
TREPANS · ROT · IAN · SOJAS
LURE · HANKYPANKY · CUE
MATSU · TOR · PIR · ABUSES
ABEAM · HOCUSPOCUS · EREBUS
TERN · LETSGO · HRH · ARLINE
HEMS · HOWDYDOODY · EUR
OCARINA · ASTHE · ELI · ASPS
CAROLINAS · IMET · ENOL
ADESTE · HIGGLEDYPIGGLEDY
LESSON · ADORE · IRAN · RINSE
ATTENT · HEROD · TOWS · ENACT
```

11

```
POSTOFFICE · ALB · INAPOT
HEARNOEVIL · HOLESINONE
LAUNDERMATS · TOUCHANDGO
DELFT · ADONAIS · TEL · GASES
EMA · ALT · ROTGUT · SETA
FONDAS · DAVINCIS · CORDOBA
INGENUES · OOHED · TRAILER
CAIRA · ACTON · ARABIA · ODRA
IDUN · MUSES · SNAKECHARMER
TEM · FIX · LLOYDC · RISE · ATA
LON · OFOURSKINS · ODIST
YANGTZE · TIU · SAMPLED
TWEED · CARSONCITY · AUG
OAS · LAHR · AFGHAN · SYS · MAW
PHIBETAKAPPA · LOCHS · FAVI
PICA · BISTRO · ISTOO · AUDEN
ONANOAK · TICKS · TOWNSEND
SENSATO · UNKNOWNS · OTSEGO
RSVP · SEISHU · UGH · YEW
SHAMS · SHE · TSCALES · OMERS
KISSMEKATE · HELLISHNESS
YESTERYEAR · ELEEMOSYNA
ERNANI · OLE · SENDINGSET
```

12

```
MASS · PALM · CAPH · RALSTON
ANIL · EQUI · SAMOA · ELEMENT
EDDO · RUNSACROSS · FINITES
DEVILANDDANIELWEBSTER
TOWATER · IMRE · EERIE
AWAKE · INDIA · OUTRE · SHAWL
RNS · SPUR · TBARS · ENC · AREA
ASHE · SMOLT · FANS · COSTING
LET · LOOKIT · OVERHEATS
OPALS · FLU · ENE · RIFTED
CALYPSO · BEE · DEERE · SOI
UPINYOURFUNKANDWAGNALLS
LAT · ORION · EWA · MEANIES
OUTLAY · STE · COE · PUDGY
CLAMSHELL · ATESTS · GAR
LEVERET · EARL · CRIME · ADDA
AMEN · STU · FRESH · EELS · IAN
PASSU · ENCRE · NEARS · OPART
PORTA · CARL · STOOGES
CROSSWORDPUZZLEMAKERS
GUANACO · HORIZONTAL · SANS
ANNULAR · OTARY · ECTO · IMOU
MANSARD · POMS · WHEN · ESTE
```

13

```
ANISE     PASHA   KILN    WASP
MEGILP    TINEAR  USIA    IXIA
MONDAYMORNING     KIBITZERS
   STRAINS  DUELS  NEA
MAW   EARLS  ASAMA    STRATA
INES  MAS  SLOBS  BLOODRED
STEPOUT  GHOUL  AROON  MED
HIKERS  QUARTERBACK  ACTE
AGENT  TUANS  OINK  OTHER
PUNT  SHIRT  BATED  SPEARS
SAD  ITOLDYOUSO    THETIS
  WISENTS  TRI  STAINER
 SAVING  CRITICISMS  GAS
MERINO  COHAN  DRESS  REVE
IRREG  MANU  SLANE  MANET
RAID  POSTMORTEMS  REVERT
APO  MOLTO  BEARS  SEVERAL
GERBILLE  RESTS  SOV  SAGE
ESSENE  BELIE  SABER  LED
  AIM  CUPID  MARINER
HINDSIGHT  SECONDGUESSES
ORAL  COAT  KNIVES  ELVERS
SKYE  SAPS  STEER   SPARS
```

14

```
PEST  SCAMP  TBAR    SPUD
ASHE  CANOE  EERY    OHARE
SPONSORSMESSAGE   SANDE
TYE  TREE  LASSO  OILSUP
   ERNS  BINET  CURT
APPLES  KONER  ARTISTRY
CRAMP  PROGRAMMERS  RAE
RIMS  SOIE   OISE  DANA
AMP  NEWSREPORTS  LINER
BEHOOVES  RUNNY  RINSES
  LATER  CONES  SEMEL
SEEKER  NOSIR  SCANDALS
KATES  TELECASTERS  TOP
ATEN  IODO  PONS  LOCI
TEE  INPANTOMIME  CORAL
ERRORHAS  ONETO  TUSSLE
  BRER  STEMS  SURE
LABOUR  TOTUP  AMBI  SOU
EQUIP  TELEPHONEBOOTHS
WURST  ITER  ISTLE  NINE
DIRT  MESS  SCALD  TROD
```

15

```
THEMAN   SADSACK  ALSACE
THEVIEW  AREOLAE  DENIALS
REMATCH  LAPLATA  JOURNAL
ICAN  IOWE  TOLA  GONG  DIA
PAT  RACIST  UNTRUE  PINT
OVINE  ANMAKE  DIOR  TIDES
DECAMP  SARAHS  CONSOLES
  VEEP  NOTATE  METRO
SOLITARY  CAREEN  DISTAL
APIE  RIOTS  DELOS  NOESIS
LETS  LOGE  STREWING  DAMP
TNT  RUNSTHERISK   WEA
USED  FIRSTAID  STOA  MEAD
SERENE  TEAIN  REELS  OLDE
 ASSESS  SINGLE  RECALLED
  PETES  RESOLE  SUSA
 TRIDENTS  DEBATE  SCRIMP
CHESS  TIER  ASYIST  OSCAR
REVE  BILLET  SOTHAT  ORA
ILE  MIME  ARAB  LEES  SMIT
MALTESE  SMETANA  EPICENE
EMERSON  LEVERET  DILATED
BRYAN  ORIENTE  UCATOR
```

16

```
RADARS  GARAGES   CESURA
ACETIC  UNALERT  LIENOR
NECTAR  NATATOR  EGRESS
ODE  NIBBLES  DINAH  ATE
FIRSTBLOOD  SEVENTHSON
FANE  BURG  TONER  BEEVE
  PELEE  CHAT  OMEI
SUTLER  THIRST  OLDAGE
IMPELS  NEARS  RATLINES
MARTS  SIPID  PACES  ANT
PROS  SECONDSIGHT  AGUA
UTA  FEWER  EPPIE  MERIT
TERRAINS  UGRIC  TIRANE
ERSATZ  TERRET  BECAME
  SHEP  AGEE  RELET
ABUSE  AGREE  BETE  ESSE
PAPERMILLS  LASTGOSPEL
TIR  TERAI  PONIERS  RID
ELICIT  MEDICAL  ATTUNE
SESAME  ISOLATE  PIECER
TEETER  STEELED  HATERS
```

17

```
ABOMA  CUTUP  RSTAR  POONA
IONIC  ALOMA  AERIE  ALLOT
DUTCHUNCLES   FRENCHLEAVE
ATOE  NOEL  TAFFY  TELAMON
      TIER  TOPIS  BORS
PLANETS  PARIS  HARD  HAHA
HERESY  CUBANHEELS  ARRET
RAGES  CANAL  ILL  PEARL
AGED  ONIC  PORPOISE  BOA
SUN  ASCOT  SUM  OVERLIES
YET  SPANISHBAYONET  EAST
   ITER  VIR  NEF  OBAN
SANE  ABIESIRISHROSE  NOG
CREATION  KAS  EARED  IRE
ROB  INSTATES  CANT  AGIN
ILEDE  ERA  ERRIS  ICHOR
PLEAD  BRAZILNUTS  DOTTLE
TAFT  TRIM  NUDES  TRUSSES
    PRAM  ISNOT  REIS
SEABEES  BLUER  POPE  ALEE
ENGLISHPEER  SIAMESECATS
CORIN  LIANE  EMCEE  GROUT
SWIPE  YOKED  SPEOS  GENIE
```

18

```
BLAS  SCRUB  SLEEP  HAMS
RAGA  PHONO  CURSE  ALOT
IGOR  RASOUMOVSKY  BENE
TONALITY  TIN  TETRAGON
     BANS  MINCE  ROAN
GESANG  SEQUENT  NIELLO
APING  VIRUS  GAP  DRIED
MEED  PADRE  ALSOP  AERO
BEG  ALLEY  BRITTEN  BON
ASMODEUS  PARSE  SOBEIT
EROSE  TORAH  FARES
FRIARS  SEPOY  CANTATAS
LOS  NIELSEN  MOUTH  RIP
ACTE  SMUTS  CARSE  CASE
SCENT  ERA  MONET  THULE
HARRIS  STRAUSS  CHIMED
   ATTS  EAGRE  SEAN
TRAVIATA  MOA  SPARRING
HONI  TRIOSONATAS  ECON
ETAS  EAGLE  TRITE  SETA
METH  SPUDS  ERRED  TRET
```

19

```
GEMINI  SPEC  LAMAR  COSMO
LEONID  KINO  ABABE  OSCAR
ERODES  INTRAVENUS  SMART
NINER  SPURNS  TESTAMENTS
NEON  SAPPY  PATTE  MINTY
   TEMPLES  HEXES  DECA
CRO  YEAR  BORED  LEER  TSE
HUNDRED  SORAS  SABREJETS
ABOARD  GILA  POST  LUNIK
FLUSH  RENDEZVOUS  CITOLE
FESS  DANK  OILS  CHEERER
   OOZE  SMOCK  CHEF
COSTUME  SEAM  BOAZ  ECHO
OPIATE  SPLASHDOWN  ETHER
SERIF  DUAL  OURS  ASCEND
BRELOQUES  HERON  NOTHERE
YEN  RUST  HANDS  BENE  SIR
   ALIT  FALSE  CELESTE
CANAL  ALIBI  MALLS  AQUA
CALCULATOR  GOODLY  GLUTS
ALTON  MOONINDIGO  BREATH
BLANC  ANDES  DREW  YANKEE
SARAH  TESTA  SERS  ASTERN
```

20

```
COPAL  ISTLE  OHARA  AHALF
ABODE  BORIS  DORIC  RUBAL
NECESSARYFORONEPEOPLETO
ESKS  TRUST  ORONO  VALLEY
SEETHE  SQUAM  RASSE  SEND
   TEARS  UPLAY  STORM
ENV  VIOLA  INES  EMMA  PAY
THEDECLARATION  SEASTOBE
RETIA  ABED  AMUR  SKULLS
EBOATS  OSIS  GAMUT  LIES
   LIPAR  EELS  CIRE  ESSE
THATTOSECURETHESERIGHTS
REDO  RIRE  AERO  STENO
ANON  TASTE  DASH  DVORAK
UNSEWS  EGAD  RHAP  ASANE
MASSACRE  OFINDEPENDENCE
ASE  RAIN  STLO  LEDGE  TEL
   NSTAR  SEGAL  EARTO
STAG  TAMES  MOPED  ISREAL
TAGORE  ONIUM  ODETO  AARE
OURFORTUNESANDOURSACRED
AREAS  BREVE  SAUCE  GETTO
TIERS  ASSES  ALTES  ASHEN
```

21

```
RACER  BLAB  BARAS  ABAS
AMOLE  AIDA  EDILE  PONT
JOURNEYTOTHEMOON  ORDO
  ROOST  SEEP  FROGMEN
EASY  THE  REGET  WEARE
ODE  THEGUMDROP  TEENSY
MASSE  MONAS  MURAS
  TOPCHOICE  APRIL  DRAT
IFI  BOSS  GREENCHEESE
  THANT  COARSE  ELATE
CAPTOR  BOOTS  DRAMAS
ALLIN  OTIOSE  CAROL
PLANETPROBE  TORE  UTE
TANG  RIATA  SECTIONED
  PEELE  CANOF  RESIN
LANDIS  ASTRONAUTS  TNT
OLEAN  ASTHE  SLY  LEAS
VITREUM  EERO  DRIED
ECHE  PUTASPIDERONMOON
LIER  OSAGE  NERO  DOURA
LARS  NEWTS  DRIP  ONTOP
```

22

```
SNUB  PIER  CATO  CHIMES
ATHENE  ANNOTATOR  LENORE
BROTHERCANYOUSPAREADIME
BARTERS  EARL  SCOOP  LIP
ADELE  MEDALS  SALON  BENE
  EDH  MUDS  CHIEF  PARED
ETCS  ADITS  HEIL  SCAR
THO  GLORY  CARES  ARAMIS
ARI  REIS  ARLES  HANK  ARA
TENSEST  CLEFS  AORTA  KID
SETAE  MATED  ALONG  LESE
PENNYWISEPOUNDFOOLISH
PESO  AIRER  LINES  ADDLE
ANT  LURES  ULNAR  BONSOIR
ICE  APES  FRATS  HOVE  UNA
DERIVE  CLARA  SOLES  GET
  DARK  AILS  RUMOR  OHNO
STIES  OGLES  DELE  TEN
ERNS  BRIAR  SUTURE  SABAL
RID  PEART  PERI  RISSOLE
AFOOLANDHISMONEYARESOON
PLOVER  LENTICULA  ANITRA
HERATS  EADS  SEAM  NESS
```

23

```
ICEAGE  TRAIT  PADUA
THEBES  TOESTHE  TURNSA
METROS  ARCHAEOLOGISTS
ORIAL  ERST  LOSES  LORS
STO  ONATOOT  PIT  PLUIE
SNUGASA  RISEN  ROALDS
  VIXENS  NAR  OUST
  PESOS  PICKANDSHOVEL
MARATS  SERAI  EDS  OILA
ULO  SIMPLON  DREE  TRAP
SARG  OREN  NOES  HUTS
IBAR  OLIO  CANITBE  SEE
NOTA  LIT  GAZED  EXCESS
GRAVELDEPOSIT  ATHOS
  EVAS  HAT  SILTUP
DOONES  SATUP  FOEMANS
ORRIS  PAS  PENNERA  OTT
REAM  MELEE  LIES  TERRA
EXCAVATIONSITE  MINOAN
NILGAI  CUSTARD  LOCATE
SEELS  TENSE  ANYDAY
```

24

```
CREPT  DECAP  DAMPS  WHATA
ROBER  ORIBI  ASNAP  HADUP
AGORA  WIDEN  MAORI  OPINE
SUNKMONK  CHOPPERHOPPER
HEYS  STS  TUAN  QUEASY
  UPTO  EARLET  ADIPOSE
SIMPLEWIMPLE  ARA  ASANOX
INE  MONTI  STABAT  PERI
DESIGN  ELF  ICESIN  APODS
IZAR  EVER  FARCRY  BYBIT
  AGILE  YBARRA  TIA  ONE
PERKYTURKEY  PALLIDSALAD
OLE  RES  ORGEAT  OMAHA
TASSE  IMABUM  ERLE  AMAH
STOPS  VOLUME  ROI  CESARE
HILL  BELAYS  STOOD  LIL
ONEIDA  ESE  VENIALMENIAL
TESTERS  ROOMIE  DELA
  STEEPS  STEP  AMU  PROB
KIPPERSHIPPER  MOPYHOPI
ADARS  TOTER  GAROU  ATTAR
RECIT  ETUDE  EWELL  WHORL
LETTS  TOPSY  SKYED  PARTS
```

25

```
ACCOSTS  PACAS  PIASTER
SHOUTAT  IRANI  IMMERGE
SANTAFE  TRENTONPERIOD
ORC  STEPHENAUSTIN  PIR
BLOCH  PLOT  PATES  SOSO
EIRE  ALUM  COTES  MALTS
REDROVER  AHLEN  VALISE
GEOID  BRAID  PAGE
SCRAPS  BEERS  COLUMBUS
COALS  CANAL  POLES  ONE
RAPS  LITTLEROCKS  ASIA
UTE  LORIS  SAMOS  ATTAR
BISMARCK  STIPA  PILOTS
AINE  CHOSE  MORAN
LAMINA  PHONE  LAMENTED
ABELE  VIEWS  BATE  TENO
TASS  TOEYE  RICH  CARTS
ELA  WALTERRALEIGH  REA
ROBERTLANSING  LOAFING
ANIMARE  NUDGE  DEPLETE
LESSPAY  EPEES  ASSURES
```

26

```
GROG  JOCKO  POCUS  CAJOLE
REMO  USHAK  IRANI  PRUNED
AGNI  THEYALEBULLDOGSONG
SLINKS  PER  DIKE  ATREE
SEATO  TIBIA  FIT  NOLA
OHHELL  DARN  PADISHAH
LITTLEMISSBLUEBIRD  HULA
ARAH  FPA  HAIG  ICY  GAMOW
MEMENTO  MACC  IDO  DIDOES
INAWAY  MONKEYS  TWOFERS
AERIE  JAR  BOLA  AUTO
SEAL  BONNYBLUEFLAG  NATO
DIRE  SEAU  OAF  LTCOL
RUBBISH  ATECROW  BOHEME
BALLET  UGH  GOAT  ROBERTA
ADEUX  TRA  POLK  AER  BROS
NAME  WHOBLEWOUTTHEFLAME
GRAYDAWN  ERNS  AMADOU
OONA  VIM  SAXON  XEBEC
PAINT  CHAS  MUD  MYSORE
ANDDARKBLUEISHEREE  IRON
STEERA  AURIC  OVERT  DAST
SHARDS  REESE  CADIZ  EXES
```

27

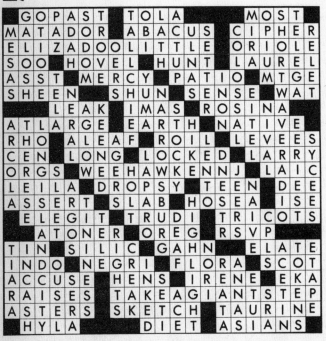

```
GOPAST  TOLA  MOST
MATADOR  ABACUS  CIPHER
ELIZADOOLITTLE  ORIOLE
SOO  HOVEL  HUNT  LAUREL
ASST  MERCY  PATIO  MTGE
SHEEN  SHUN  SENSE  WAT
LEAK  IMAS  ROSINA
ATLARGE  EARTH  NATIVE
RHO  ALEAF  ROIL  LEVEES
CEN  LONG  LOCKED  LARRY
ORGS  WEEHAWKENNJ  LAIC
LEILA  DROPSY  TEEN  DEE
ASSERT  SLAB  HOSEA  ISE
ELEGIT  TRUDI  TRICOTS
ATONER  OREG  RSVP
TIN  SILIC  GAHN  ELATE
INDO  NEGRI  FLORA  SCOT
ACCUSE  HENS  IRENE  EKA
RAISES  TAKEAGIANTSTEP
ASTERS  SKETCH  TAURINE
HYLA  DIET  ASIANS
```

28

```
ABRASE  BELA  POET  APTS
CUEMAN  HURON  BURRO  WART
ESSOIN  ERICA  ASTROLOGER
THEICEMANCOMETH  ELEME
WED  AIDES  THEPACE  BOA
OSAR  CORONAE  SOSO  DORM
NEHRU  NEWSPAPERBOYS
TOOSMOOTH  ILIA  PAROL
AWN  MTN  ENT  ALLY  ESCARP
JESTER  POH  NEA  ASSEGAI
ATO  RAGES  SOUPY  ORE
BONG  DOCTORZHIVAGO  AGED
UNI  ADLAI  IOLES  NOB
LESACRE  CPO  VEG  DUETTO
GRIGRI  FAIN  EDA  BET  OUR
LIVRE  LEAR  STANDERBY
THEDEERSLAYER  HITON
TROT  RENO  CARAMEL  ATTS
RIM  ASKSFOR  NICEA  HIC
IBEAM  THEBEGGARSOPERA
NURSERYMEN  ARENT  FLORAL
ANUT  ADANO  SIREE  AIDEDE
LENO  PSTS  TEST  TOSSER
```

29

```
IDAS  MOPSA      REDBEAR
NOME  ARRETE   IDEAMEN
EDWIN GROWINGUPABSURD
LUNGING  SENNAS  MIS
SCHOLA OID EVAN  TOUTS
ATI ERASTUS  EGAL  SNEE
SELS IFS  PHILEMON DSC
ELEVATED  ETE  EXEGETE
SADE ETA  SIDED  DORAD
LUNAR  NATO  SRI  ETTE
FALLOFTHEHOUSEOFUSHER
UNTO  THM  MOST  PARSE
NAHUA  ESTOP  LAP  ALBS
CRESTOF ESS  OVERLOOK
HEW TRAPNETS  IRE  WAIF
ATAT ALEE  OPPOSER  RTE
LAYOF  LABS  EON  VENDRE
PUP  CROTAL  RENEWAL
HIGHERTHANAKITE  AVAIS
UNOARED  TOUCHE  TELL
BIGTOPS  SPEED  ARKS
```

30

```
AMORET  COMO  SAGA  PORES
LAMINA  AVERS  EVIL  ASANA
TRIALBALANCE  DOLLARSIGN
OCT ABILL  ARTICLES  AMID
NOSTRILS  VALE  EPI  ENE
AGEE  CABINETS  IRONED
UNCLES  TONAL  PARENTS
ROUES  SIMOLEON  IDEST
SETS SELENE  TONNER  APIS
ALA  SENT  TRIES  CREDO
MOLASSES  CEDES  RAINED
ELEVATE  CALORIC  BANANAS
RELETS  BORED  CEREMONY
ODORS  COLON  OLPE  WHF
SANS TALENT  STEALS  BIOL
TOAST  GOLCONDA  FOSSA
STELLAE  AULIS  PALEST
CARPAL  DECANTED  ARLO
AMA  SES  MING  CLASSPIN
LAVO SERENADE  BELIE  IRI
CREDITCARD  ONEASYSTREET
AIRED  CAGE  NORIA  ETERNE
RASSE  ODER  SEER  DOSSER
```

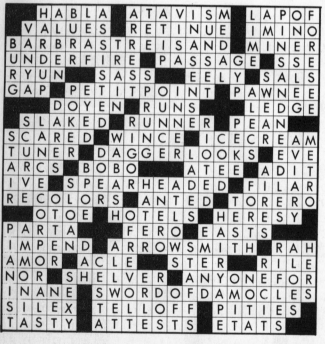

31

```
HABLA  ATAVISM  LAPOF
VALUES  RETINUE  IMINO
BARBRASTREISAND  MINER
UNDERFIRE  PASSAGE  SSE
RYUN  SASS  EELY  SALS
GAP PETITPOINT  PAWNEE
DOYEN  RUNS  LEDGE
SLAKED  RUNNER  PEAN
SCARED  WINCE  ICECREAM
TUNER  DAGGERLOOKS  EVE
ARCS BOBO  ATEE  ADIT
IVE SPEARHEADED  FILAR
RECOLORS  ANTED  TORERO
OTOE  HOTELS  HERESY
PARTA  FERO  EASTS
IMPEND  ARROWSMITH  RAH
AMOR  ACLE  STER  RILE
NOR SHELVER  ANYONEFOR
INANE SWORDOFDAMOCLES
SILEX  TELLOFF  PITIES
TASTY  ATTESTS  ETATS
```

32

```
TOADS   BRO  IRANIC  ASAD
OMNIUM HOED  SENORA  RODE
PAYDAYWAYLAYNAYSAY  EMAN
OHMY OAT  SOCS  ISOGENS
PAODE  REGALE  HUBS  DAFOE
SHROP  ADIREFIREWIRE
HAE TEEVEES  ROTA  ANDWOE
OHM SOCIAL  BAR  VBS  WIN
PAIR NOT  AMI  SEAT  MILT
NEW  NAE  AGT  PWR  HALSE
WHITECOLLARDOLLARHOLLER
HEMIDEMISEMIQUAVERSAVER
ALONGSIDETOGUIDETHERIDE
TODAY  CON  TRE  SST  SIE
HIES PALE  ISA  ASB  AWNS
ASS  ELI  SAG  DEVOTE  WOE
SEISMO DREW  MAKEFUN  HRE
MAINPLANELANE  AGOOD
LIMNS  EENS  ERASED  MOLEY
ANOTHER  AIMS  EEE  ALAD
PURA ACOBBLEJOBLLWOBBLE
USAF  THRILL  IDES  ARIOSE
PELE SETTEE  GET  STOOD
```

33

```
JUTS  RACED  EBOND  SMEW
ANAK  ETHAN  VINCE  OUZO
URBI  THEVANITYOF  FEIN
NUL  THOSE  ILEX  LLANOS
THEWORST  ACES  PAIRS
TARO  EAGER  ARTISTIC
CHAIRWARMER  FLOE  OENO
HELLS  STER  BLOB  AGRON
ARKS  DUOS  CLOSERTO
SEE  HORN  RHEAS  ATOLLS
SORBILE  FOIST  DIEDOUT
ENSURE  RIANT  BONN  UGO
RESPONSE  DEWY  SNAP
CASED  HUNT  SIDE  LIGNI
ALMA  LAGS  STOOLPIGEON
PLEURISY  SCARF  ROIL
ACUTE  COUP  RUINLIKE
GARRET  SOLD  VOLES  ZEP
AMIA  LAMPOONISTS  MANO
ZINC  EROSE  ALERT  ORYX
EDGY  RAGED  MESAS  DDAY
```

34

```
SAGES  SAMBA  RESAW  CACTI
CURLY  TRAIL  OSELA  ARLES
ADAMSNEEDLE  JACKSONCENT
LIN  TONSIL  EAU  AHSO  VOL
POTIONS  SEMIS  ALIS  MERE
IDLE  LOTUS  CLINICAL
ANNEE  FIN  REDOING  ALAMO
MOAN  VARAN  NUGGET  RENEW
INITIATIVE  HRON  OPPIDAN
RADICLE  EOZOON  ENSEMBLE
CHI  INLAW  SWEDE  PAIR
CST  SAJOU  GEM  INCUR  YES
ATRI  NONES  REPLY  DAB
SOUTACHE  MAJLIS  MORELLO
ALMADEN  LIRA  MOTIVATION
BEALE  STERIC  ANITA  TNUT
ANNIE  OATCAKE  SLY  RECTO
CAMENIGH  ETAPE  CERO
ARAN  IGLO  STALE  TUSSLED
SOP  HERS  PES  STUART  NMU
HOOVERAPRON  HARRISONRED
ESTER  SINUS  OCEAN  REESE
STEED  SNARE  CELLO  EDDAS
```

35

```
REPASTE  LIEDER  DACHA
ELECTED  ANGRIER  AGUES
CAPTIVEAUDIENCE  TARAS
LITANY  TRUSS  EYRE  TRI
ANA  GESTES  SAD  ERSATZ
MELD  SEAL  ACCESS  WISE
ESKER  TRELLIS  OATEN
MILS  DIOR  INTHERED
SPIGOTS  PACING  ITALY
VIE  ASHEN  FLORA  OLIVE
IMAS  TELEG  ELAND  YSER
LINER  SAURY  ARDOR  ERS
MAUVE  THREES  EDUCERS
ANTENNAS  ALOP  ARTY
GRIEG  ASPIRIN  SACCO
ALAE  HEAVES  ORCA  SLOP
FOLDER  SAP  FRIERS  ELP
FUL  BURT  AGUAS  MAGALO
ODETO  BEHINDTHESCENES
RERUN  IRONAGE  CORTEGE
DRYAD  NETTED  AFEARED
```

36

```
AVOIDS  RAINS  OFFA  FIRMS
CATNIP  INTOW  NAIL  ASHOT
MARSEILLAISE  SUNBONNETS
ELA  STULMS  EMEND  UBOAT
FREE  STETS  BTES
DAV  BIAS  TOILS  BILLYJOE
INEVERY  BURSE  SEEIT  UPA
AGNATE  EARTHENWARE  SPIT
DEULS  ANNES  AONE  WHINE
ELSE  PRATE  AEROS  WHITEN
MAS  NEPTUNESCUP  THERES
FLORAE  TAR  BOILER
ALLIED  MERCURYLAMP  SCS
MAYORS  TEREK  HEADS  EBON
ARTYS  ARAG  PENNY  SCENE
NORD  PLUTOCRATIC  LECAMA
SNA  FROES  ROTOS  MITERED
ESPALIER  GAMER  DASH  DNS
TOSS  ALTAR  LENT
METOO  PREEN  LISTED  MAT
SATURNALIA  THEMOONSTONE
PRUNE  REAM  ICANT  TCARTS
TINED  MASS  CANSO  OSAGES
```

37

CRESS · MESH · BESTS
SHUTUP · DACHA · WALKING
PENCILPUSHER · ARMINARM
URN · TARS · OLDTIMES · PEA
DRIP · TOTS · FRATER · BRAT
SYNOD · PENS · OPEN · WROTE
GNAT · RUMPLED · CHILLS
SAWDUST · BILLS · FREELY
ALA · BAIT · LOS · GRIEF
ROTC · REUSED · DOUBLINGS
AHEAD · PRAY · ROTI · SNARE
HARROWING · YACHTS · GROW
RAINS · DEN · SELF · RAE
SWILLS · COAST · DIAMOND
UPHOLD · FOGHORN · PLOW
POOLS · BLUE · MEOW · LAMBS
BILE · FRYPAN · SWIG · NILE
OLE · PHIBETES · ISNT · NUN
WELLTODO · DRESSPARADES
ROYALLY · OVATE · SURETE
TEHEE · GARY · HEADS

38

ANGLE · RIATA · HADES · ADAGE
FORAY · ONRED · ADULT · DIVAN
ALICEISLAND · NELLANDVOID
RATE · TAEL · SADLY · RELENTS
DART · PURSE · ASWE
NASTILY · CAPRA · AVIS · UMBO
INAWAY · PATTYWAGON · CAIRN
CORAL · TANTO · HIC · ARNIE
ERAS · ONCE · FLANAGAN · NAG
NAH · AMUSE · PIE · DARTLING
EKE · BERYLLINGALONG · CESS
NEAR · EEL · ALI · OILS
MADS · CLARAFICATIONS · KIM
ERITREAN · ELY · ABUSE · INE
DAP · ARCATURE · GNAT · ERST
ABIES · EOS · HAIRS · ACTII
LITUP · EMMAGRATES · SECEDE
SAYS · DAIS · LUNES · SCOLDER
ORRA · BONDS · ETON
STAPLES · MUSTY · AVER · POSH
HELENWHEELS · MARIANHASTE
ALONE · OSAGE · ALACK · ARSON
NATTY · TOTED · NESTS · DROPS

39

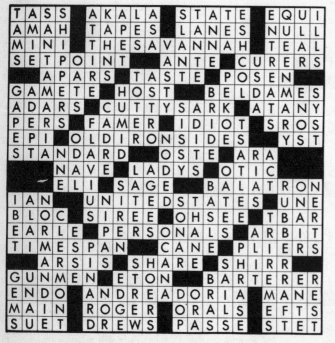

TASS · AKALA · STATE · EQUI
AMAH · TAPES · LANES · NULL
MINI · THESAVANNAH · TEAL
SETPOINT · ANTE · CURERS
APARS · TASTE · POSEN
GAMETE · HOST · BELDAMES
ADARS · CUTTYSARK · ATANY
PERS · FAMER · IDIOT · SROS
EPI · OLDIRONSIDES · YST
STANDARD · OSTE · ARA
NAVE · LADYS · OTIC
ELI · SAGE · BALATRON
IAN · UNITEDSTATES · UNE
BLOC · SIREE · OHSEE · TBAR
EARLE · PERSONALS · ARBIT
TIMESPAN · CANE · PLIERS
ARSIS · SHARE · SHIRR
GUNMEN · ETON · BARTERER
ENDO · ANDREADORIA · MANE
MAIN · ROGER · ORALS · EFTS
SUET · DREWS · PASSE · STET

40

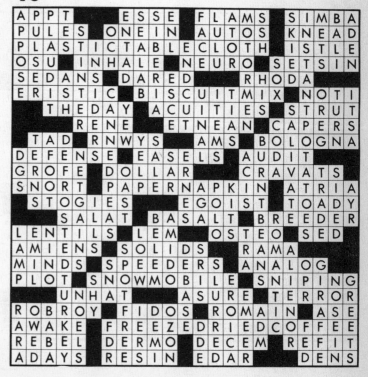

APPT · ESSE · FLAMS · SIMBA
PULES · ONEIN · AUTOS · KNEAD
PLASTICTABLECLOTH · ISTLE
OSU · INHALE · NEURO · SETSIN
SEDANS · DARED · RHODA
ERISTIC · BISCUITMIX · NOTI
THEDAY · ACUITIES · STRUT
RENE · ETNEAN · CAPERS
TAD · RNWYS · AMS · BOLOGNA
DEFENSE · EASELS · AUDIT
GROFE · DOLLAR · CRAVATS
SNORT · PAPERNAPKIN · ATRIA
STOGIES · EGOIST · TOADY
SALAT · BASALT · BREEDER
LENTILS · LEM · OSTEO · SED
AMIENS · SOLIDS · RAMA
MINDS · SPEEDERS · ANALOG
PLOT · SNOWMOBILE · SNIPING
UNHAT · ASURE · TERROR
ROBROY · FIDOS · ROMAIN · ASE
AWAKE · FREEZEDRIEDCOFFEE
REBEL · DERMO · DECEM · REFIT
ADAYS · RESIN · EDAR · DENS

41

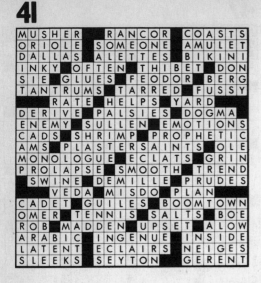

```
MUSHER  RANCOR  COASTS
ORIOLE  SOMEONE AMULET
DALLAS  ALETTES BIKINI
INKY OFTEN THIBET DON
SIE GLUES FEODOR BERG
TANTRUMS TARRED FUSSY
RATE HELPS YARD
DERIVE PALSIES DOGMA
ENEMY SULLEN EMOTIONS
CADS SHRIMP PROPHETIC
AMS PLASTERSAINTS OLE
MONOLOGUE ECLATS GRIN
PROLAPSE SMOOTH TREND
SWINE DEMILLE PRUDES
VEDA MISDO PLAN
CADET GUILES BOOMTOWN
OMER TENNIS SALTS BOE
ROB MADDEN UPSET ALOW
ARABIC INGENUE INSIDE
LATENT ECLAIRS NEIGES
SLEEKS SEYTON GERENT
```

42

```
COEDS ASPEN SWATSAT FTS
ONTAP SNIDE HASHISH AHA
ZENDA CONES ASTENSE CIR
DADDYIWANTADIAMONDRING
YEO PRI NELL SIENNA
SOLIDGOLDCADILLAC EDGES
AMA ARO URN LOP RUSS
ANITA AWHALE ABELE OPTO
RICHEST AUSABLEFORKS
ENTERED AFT RELEASE
CHIC ADA ESTS EMS ESSEX
HIGHLY MINKSTOLE DEFINE
ALLIA APT APEX ABO OATS
STUNNED SAL ITNEVER
CANDYISDANDY REDMANS
FISH ASONE LEERAT SETUP
ASTI SUR FLU CHE ONE
RIALS PEARLOFGREATPRICE
ANGLER PAON AIT TOO
PLEASESIRIWANTSOMEMORE
AIM ALAMODE AHAND AMISH
RNA MARINER MELES DENSE
TEN EXETERS ERASE EDGAR
```

43

```
MAIDS NAPA ALOP REBAR
INSET IRONCLADS EARLE
SOLER MOONLANDINGSITE
SLADES SHOULD EREBUS
YEN APSE MAG WEE ESE
DEMIT IMP READER
SPUN TERNES AMI TAMPA
TEND SEATS ENCL SPOOL
ADIME PRESENTEES TULE
RAVED SER VICEROY NYC
LENES CREDO PASTE
AIR RACCOON LOA LEASH
LEST CORNSTALKS UNITE
TREES RUTS BERLE SNEW
ASSET ASI NOGOOD ERRS
SULLEN ERE PIEDA
BAM DAS ELA FELT IDS
OREADS NEROLI EARLET
REALESTATEAGENT PEWEE
ACTOR HEARTLINE ENARM
HAYES ORLY ERST STYES
```

44

```
SCAPA QUIT WHILOM SHOE
HAVOC UNTO HECATE HENRY
ILIAC ADEL IRONON EXTRA
FLA OGLE ASCEND TIP HAP
TANTRUM MUCH PITH ETE
ODA DEGUST ELOGE GUS
FORHIMHATHTHINNENOROOME
ORION OVI SALADA EDH
RET GOBIES LESE ASSORTS
AGATTU DROLL AMAT WHEAT
ROSA ROBB IRISH ELL
CHRISTMASEVEISCOMEANDLO
HOI ASIDE ETRE ECTO
OBOLI TERM ORATE THWART
POTENCY VISA MALAYA ZOO
NTH FICKLE BIT VROUW
ONESMALLCHILDFROMHEAVEN
FAR AQUAE SPIRIT AYN
AVE TUNG ELIZ QUETSCH
TAW TEA VETOED GATS ARE
UHHUH TIESUP ADIT ELCID
BOONE ISRAEL YOGA EARED
SNOW CAYUSE STIR NYASA
```

45

```
SLAP OBEYS BAYS FORA
LOLA FUGUE GALOP AMIS
ABOLTFROMTHEBLUE DECK
VAGARIES TINES CHINKS
TENN RINDS TION
PAGING SINGE BRAGGART
AMIND FINGERNAILS SOI
NOVE SAGS URNS SCUP
TRI ONTHESQUARE MORES
SENTRIES LUNGE OATEN
GOADS BOITE ARROW
STOLE CRETE EMBALLED
BAHTS DOESONESBIT ORE
RUES MEED ATIT SOIE
IDA SAWDAYLIGHT BUSED
MIXTURES AIDES DURESS
AVID SNEER ORIG
GOTHAM TACNA STYLISTS
ALUI BURIESTHEHATCHET
MINT ATANY EARED AONE
YOGI SEPT SPARS LEST
```

46

```
CRS ALES JINX AME
QUICKLIME ONEANDONE
PULVERIZED INSTALLING
RAVENS ARGON GINGER
AVERT ARGENTINE BAMRA
HERS RIDE EUROPA RAGS
ART JARS STREWING SYS
ZYME PAWED LOOM
GREENS BOLOS JADEITES
RELAX HELOT PATERNITY
ABEL PERIPHERIES AMUR
DEMOCRATS RAILS CREDO
SLITHERS LERES THESES
SIFT KEELS DIET
SAC CAITIFFS SUEZ DAS
IMAM BEATTO SPED SERT
TAROS RESOURCES CHOSE
AZALEA VRAIC TRADER
REMITTANCE GETHSEMANE
SENTENCER ENRAPTURE
LEO TOSS STEM ESS
```

47

```
FIREI TODAY WEWHO INIGO
ANAGS AMIDO AVION NOSAD
RINGA READY YELLS KAAMA
STANDINGROOMONLY BESHE
ISTOOD AYN AFTS GODHELP
GRIS ANA APO TRAP
THEPEOPLETHEMOBTHECROWD
SONO MOORES AMAH DOA
ABDUL TSIN ONEARM MYNAH
RETRIM SCOWL SLIES SONE
AETAS IRIDS LATA TEA
AHBROKENISTHEGOLDENBOWL
CAL NERO HORAS EMCEE
URET SISAL SANTA STANZA
PASHA NOSEAT DECS SLAYS
EAT NEON SHOTUP AIMS
JOSTLINGANDBEINGJOSTLED
ARTO NUS FUN ISEE
SNOWMAN PERM QUA ITCAME
EPEES MYCUPRUNNETHOVER
EVORA LEROI SATAN IMALL
TENON ADULT VSIGN TEHEE
CRAFT POSES PILES ERIES
```

48

```
PLATINUM SLOB TROUTS
PROVOLONE LAVA HISSAT
REVERENCE IRED INHERE
ISERE MAT DARNING ORE
MAST BASIC DESK ANER
AGE CON NARROWMINDED
LETSON GROANS TIES
HIER PRATE ROC NIE
AMANDA LACE LOVESONG
GRIDS TEACH FUSE PONG
ARNI BLACK TAPER IDEE
BIDE RISE VALET DELED
OVERTAKE WALL TRADED
REX HIE CELLI AERO
PEAN MELLON LINAGE
FASTTHINKING PAN DEV
MANS REST ESSAY FATE
ELD BURNETT HUM RAMON
SLICES ARAM OPERATIVE
TENANT MERE RELEGATED
ANGLES EDEN TRAVELER
```

49

```
CAPES SIRAT SCALE ATIME
OPART INUSE EAGER BONER
HARRYTRUMANCAPOTE LLAMA
ACTS HERON ALERT BALLES
NEY SANER OVERA GAZELLE
SOLI DOER AUGER
PATRICKHENRYJAMES REC
BOGOTA REGAN ELIS CLARA
ALIA CARA UNITS ROBOT
JESSEJAMESCAGNEY CERISE
ART BUSES ALLYN BLANDER
LONER HOI BLUME
ANOINTS ASONE CRANE SAM
SARNIA OTTOGRAHAMGREENE
ISLET START LANE ODER
DIODE LALA OPTIC DOSAGE
ESP EARLWARRENHARDING
BANTU GEAR NOON
CHARLIE BOGGY CLAIR BAH
HAROLD BURRO TRACT MANO
OVENS NORMANTHOMASHARDY
IRATE AIMED RICER ANGEL
RELET GLARE SNERD GEESE
```

50

```
SCOLD PARTED CHAM
STEREO ILOILO HALAS
CLARAANNFOWLER AVERTS
HERON CAFES MITRE IRA
EATS TOILS WESER SEAN
AVE THULE NANDA ONDIT
TERRIERS MANTA DHARNA
EAST ROTE YOUARE
ALLURE TOTARA ARRESTS
RAINA BASIL NITRE SIP
IDLE TULAFINKLEA BLEU
ELY CURER EELER FLEUR
LECTERN YOWLED SLURPS
HOLISM SOLD RHEE
STALIN ALTOS JOUSTING
PAULA BRAID BUNCH TON
ORCS CEIBA CRACK GETA
RAH PIANO CHINA ORRIS
TWOBIT ARCHIBALDLEACH
AISLE DERIDE LEGATE
NAYS EDITED IRATE
```